Jesus, Lord of Creation

By
Gregory L. Jackson, PhD

Illustrated
By
Norma Boeckler

Text copyright, 2010, Gregory L. Jackson
Art copyright, 2010, Norma Boeckler
ISBN# 978-1-4357-7505-3

Acknowledgements

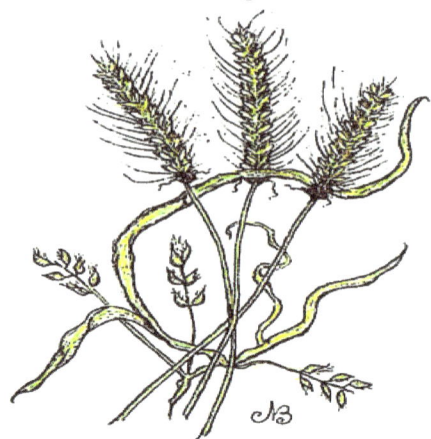

All Scriptural quotations in this book are from the King James Version of the Bible (Authorized Version) unless otherwise noted.

My wife Christina urged me to write as much as possible, patiently sewing and beading, like Penelope, through a dozen books and a dissertation.

Norma Boeckler's artistic works can be viewed at her website: (See sample below).

http://www.normaboecklerart.com

She has created a beautiful website for this book, with the same illustrations in color, at: http://0328613.netsolhost.com

Dedication

This volume is affectionately dedicated to the memory of Walter H. Boeckler, who served with great distinction as a research biologist for The Dow Chemical Company in Midland, Michigan.

Walter was born on July 28, 1931 and died December 4, 2002. Walter and his wife Norma were always devoted to the cause of the Lutheran faith as confessed in the Book of Concord. Providentially they were able to help start Holy Cross Lutheran Church in Midland.

When our independent Lutheran conference met in Midland, the families went out to dine together, a tradition we have maintained from year to year. Everyone expected to pay his own bill, which was another custom. When we prepared to pay for our food, the waitress said that was impossible. The bill was paid. My favorite memory of Walter is seeing him grinning as he relished the chance to fund our dinner. The occasion has served as a reminder of the Gospel message that everything has already been paid through the redemption of Christ.

Norma Boeckler has suffered many delays in the completion of this book, offering her artistic talent and learning website design to advance the message of Creation. This book would be almost lifeless without her inspiring and inspired artistic work.

Table of Contents

Introduction	4
The First Day	13
The Second Day	20
The Third Day	32
The Fourth Day	41
The Fifth Day	47
The Sixth Day	63
The Seventh Day	72
The Flood, Our Faith, and Science	87

Introduction

One Truth

There are many ways to consider the nature of the Holy Trinity. The Scriptures are one unified truth, revealed by God through His Holy Spirit. We can begin with any truth and examine the other truths revealed by God.

Here is an interesting contrast. How many people have thought of this?

We know Jesus is our Savior because this truth is revealed through the Scriptures. Islam is quite different. Moslems teach that Mohammed has given them the Koran, so the Koran is holy through the so-called prophet, who is considered by them to be the only and the true messenger of Allah. The moon-god of Mohammed's family was Allah. Therefore the Koran is whatever Mohammed declared it to be. He was illiterate but a talented poet. Others wrote down his verses. He included versus about Allah having daughters, due to pressure from one group that would not give up their daughter goddesses, but he later withdrew those verses and called them Satanic verses, the name of Rushdie's famous book. Therefore, in Islam, the religious book is centered around one man and his own compositions. Mohammed created a wealthy kingdom for himself by sponsoring armed raids against the caravans of other Bedouins. In contrast, Jesus had no home.

**And Jesus saith unto him, The foxes have holes, and the birds of the air *have* nests; but the Son of man hath not where to lay *his* head.
Matthew 8:20**

The Foxes

Unlike the Koran, the Scriptures come from the hands of many men and yet have a divinely-wrought consistency throughout, due to the inspiration of the Holy Spirit. The believer trusts in the inerrancy of the Bible because of the power of the Word. The Word of God teaches us so completely and compellingly about our nature and our Savior that we cannot do anything but confirm its origin and nature. Therefore, it is not surprising when we learn new bits of information dug up from the ancient past, confirming minor details recorded in the Bible. Those details were once denied with great vehemence by scoffers and skeptics but conveniently overlooked when confirmed by archeology.

A key foundational truth of the Bible is that God has instilled purpose in each and every one of us through His Creation. There are two alternative philosophies, or ways of understanding the data around us.

1) Either God created and we all have a divine purpose. Or

2) Chaos has organized itself into an orderly and self-sustaining world, purely by coincidence.

The Bible teaches that God brought order out of nothingness and chaos:

In the beginning God created the heaven and the earth. 2 And the earth was without form, and void; and darkness *was* upon the face of the deep. And the Spirit of God moved upon the face of the waters. 3 And God said, Let there be light: and there was light. 4 And God saw the light, that *it was* good: and God divided the light from the darkness. Genesis 1:1-4

In our own little world, chaos does not progress into order. Instead, order degenerates into chaos. For instance, neglect the least little chores in a home and soon it is difficult to walk through a room or put a sack of groceries on a clean counter. Desks do not organize themselves over time. Instead they become more disorderly. More papers, pen, candies, bills, tools, and computer equipment piles up until nothing can be found.

Where man has control, there must be a constant effort to keep things from declining any faster than they will on their own.

God created beavers with a need to chew constantly and to build dams. Their dams are so well built that people use dynamite to blow them up when their ponds would engulf valuable land. Beavers encourage the formation of ponds. The ponds become loaded with plant and animal life because algae grows almost instantly in the sun. Algae feeds many forms of aquatic life. Fish enter the pond through the feet of water fowl, who are programmed by God to be attracted to water and to mark it on their mental maps. When I had the waterfall splashing one evening, geese flew overhead. One seemed to be looking down for the source of the water-noise. Even a dripping bucket into another water bucket will attract birds of all kinds.

The pond created by beavers takes care of itself. The fish and plants feed, cleanse, and add nutrition to the pond. Any pond will become a center of activity. It will keep itself clean and healthy in almost all circumstances. God has life-forms for all kinds of water except the Dead Sea. Finally the pond will silt itself up and become a fertile piece of ground.

In contrast, a man-made swimming pool needs 12 hours of pumping, filtering, and chlorine each day to keep it clean in the summer. The swimming pool does not clean itself. It does not fill itself with water. Left alone, even with timers, a good power source, and an auto-filling option, it will break down and turn into an opaque mess.

This seems so clear to us. The problem is that people look at the same facts and come to different conclusions. The evolutionist sees the Grand Canyon and says, "Evolution." The Christian sees the Grand Canyon and says, "The Flood."

The evolutionist looks at religious history and says, "There must have been some big floods, because every culture has a flood story with one family surviving. Genesis probably got Noah's story from the Babylonians."

Christians look at this same history and say, "No wonder every culture has a flood story. It really happened. And the Bible does not need a source to reveal the truth to us."

Scientists can gather a vast array of facts, and we are thankful for that. But they admit that they cannot discuss purpose. The whole concept of purpose is a non-scientific concept. That is the ultimate problem of turning chaos into order by chance over billions of years. Arguing the impossibility of such occurrences is not very convincing and irrelevant to most people.

The real issue is how one can say two forms of life have a purpose, one for the other, and then multiply this by an infinite level of complexity. For example, the beaver must chew on trees to be happy and contented. He must make a dam and a nice little home for his family. All of his fellow creatures immediately benefit from his work. They need him as much as he needs the trees to chew and build with, as much as he needs the water for his pond. Fish arrive at the isolated pond because their eggs from other ponds cling to the legs of waterfowl. This gives the fish population *Lebensraum* (elbow room) and the birds more food.

If there is a pond soaking in the sun, I will show you the dragon fly family. They hover and dart over the pond, grabbing insects on the fly. No man-made aircraft has the flight control flexibility of the dragonfly. And yet there is another secret to this insect. As a baby it lives in the pond as an attack submarine, feeding as ferociously on insect larvae as it will devour mature insects in its adult stage. How many submarines can turn themselves into attack helicopters by feeding themselves on the enemy and then produce even more of these transforming insect-destroyers?

The lower forms of life – even the lifeless minerals – point to the purpose we all share as God's creation, as human beings. The rocks crumble into soil, and those minerals become building blocks of plant and animal life. The way in which all of God's Creation sustains itself is a constant marvel to everyone, although many interpret it wrongly. They rhapsodize about "Nature" and not about the Creator. They want to protect "Nature" while disparaging the Creator.

Nevertheless, we see in the inter-relatedness of Creation the sign of God's design and purpose. Creation shows us the outline so that no one can deny God, as Paul teaches:

For the invisible things of him from the creation of the world are clearly seen, being understood by the things that are made, *even* his eternal power and Godhead; so that they are without excuse: 21 Because that, when they knew God, they glorified *him* not as God, neither were thankful; but became vain in their imaginations, and their foolish heart was darkened. Romans 1:20-21

The Scriptures teach us the nature of God's purpose.

And we have known and believed the love that God hath to us. God is love; and he that dwelleth in love dwelleth in God, and God in him. 17 Herein is our love made perfect, that we may have boldness in the day of judgment: because as he is, so are we in this world. 18 There is no fear in love; but perfect love casteth out fear: because fear hath torment. He that feareth is not made perfect in love. 19 We love him, because he first loved us. 20 If a man say, I love God, and hateth his brother, he is a liar:for he that loveth not his brother whom he hath seen, how can he love God whom he hath not seen? 21 And this commandment have we from him, That he who loveth God love his brother also. 1 John 4:16-21

This is the famous passage that reveals to us the simple phrase:

God is Love

Therefore, those who dwell in God (who remain with and are faithful to the Gospel and Sacraments) dwell in love. The passage also means that lovelessness is not in harmony with faith in God.

Another simple but profound idea comes from this passage in I John:

> That we may have boldness on the day of judgment.
>
> Bold shall I stand in that great Day
> For who aught to my charge shall lay?
> Fully through these absolved I am,
> From sin and fear, from guilt and shame.
>
> "Jesus, Thy Blood and Righteousness," TLH 371

This epistle lesson shows us that God created us to live in love. First of all, He created us to live in His love. The Gospel message is a constant and unfailing message of God's love and forgiveness. We love Him because He first loved us. From that love comes our love for others. As the Apostle John notes, fear and love are opposites. Fearful people are not loving, but loving people cast out fear. It is always going to be part of our human condition, but faith nurtured in God's love casts away fear.

The reason so many laity and clergy are timid today is their lack of trust in God. Not that God is denying them anything or proving false to them. They simply do not trust God to add anything to their human cleverness. Trust in their own devices, they shudder when things do not work out.

I was talking to a university leader. She always started from a position of trusting faculty members and encouraging them. But then she was replaced by someone who tried to show his power with threats and power-plays. Faculty voted on this change by resigning, even after decades of service.

In the same way, and much more profoundly, Jesus attracts all people to Himself because of His love and mercy. Therefore, we each have a purpose in God's Kingdom. One of the best ways to show that purpose is to multiply the love which God has already shown us, to extend the forgiveness He has already given us in Christ, to live as though the promise of eternal life is our one great certainty, based upon the objective Word of God and the merits of Christ.

"Behold a Host, Arrayed in White"
by Hans A. Brorson, 1694-1764

> Behold a host, arrayed in white,
> Like thousand snow-clad mountains bright,

With palms they stand. Who is this band
Before the throne of light?
Lo, these are they of glorious fame
Who from the great affliction came
And in the flood of Jesus' blood
Are cleansed from guilt and blame.
Now gathered in the holy place,
Their voices they in worship raise,
Their anthems swell where God doth dwell,
Mid angels' songs of praise.

Despised and scorned, they sojourned here;
But now, how glorious they must appear!
Those martyrs stand a priestly band,
God's throne forever near.
So oft, in troubled days gone by,
In anguish they would weep and sigh,
At home above the God of Love
For aye their tears shall dry.
They now enjoy their Sabbath rest,
The paschal banquet of the blest;
The Lamb, their Lord, at festal board
Himself is Host and Guest.

Then hail, ye mighty legions, yea,
All hail! Now safe and blest for aye,
And praise the Lord, who with His Word
Sustained you on the way.
Ye did the joys of earth disdain,
Ye toiled and sowed in tears and pain.
Farewell, now bring your sheaves and sing
Salvation's glad refrain.
Swing high your palms, lift up your song,
Yea, make it myriad voices strong,
Eternally shall praise to Thee,
God, and the Lamb belong.

Paul the Apostle – On Creation

For I am not ashamed of the gospel of Christ: for it is the power of God unto salvation to every one that believeth; to the Jew first, and also to the Greek. 17 For therein is the righteousness of God revealed from faith to faith: as it is written, The just shall live by faith. 18 For the wrath of God is revealed from heaven against all ungodliness and unrighteousness of men, who hold the truth in

unrighteousness; 19 Because that which may be known of God is manifest in them; for God hath shewed *it* unto them.

20 For the invisible things of him from the creation of the world are clearly seen, being understood by the things that are made, *even* his eternal power and Godhead; so that they are without excuse: 21 Because that, when they knew God, they glorified *him* not as God, neither were thankful; but became vain in their imaginations, and their foolish heart was darkened. 22 Professing themselves to be wise, they became fools, 23 And changed the glory of the uncorruptible God into an image made like to corruptible man, and to birds, and fourfooted beasts, and creeping things. Romans 1:16-23.

The First Day

In the beginning God created the heaven and the earth. 2 And the earth was without form, and void; and darkness *was* upon the face of the deep. And the Spirit of God moved upon the face of the waters. 3 And God said, Let there be light: and there was light. 4 And God saw the light, that *it was* good: and God divided the light from the darkness. 5 And God called the light Day, and the darkness he called Night. And the evening and the morning were the first day. Genesis 1:1-5

Religions of the world have many different creation accounts, but only one is the revealed Word of God. In the beginning, God created. This creation is essential for understanding our lives, the world we inhabit, and the Christian faith. Each and every day we should look about and admire what the Creator has accomplished for us – from the soil teeming with microscopic life, insects, worms, reptiles, and mammals to the spangled skies above us, lit with stars, an occasional comet, and changed by the cycles of planets and our moon. Man, the paragon of all animals is the greatest wonder of Creation, with an amazing complexity of God-given intelligence, emotion, and faith.

The wise of the ages have debated the exact nature of this First Day, often in spite of the plain language of Scripture. God created out of nothing, *ex nihilo* among the theologians. Did God create this first matter, the earth which was formless, void, and dark? This is clearly answered in the Gospel of John, which declares of the Creating Word:

All things were made by him; and without him was not any thing made that was made. John 1:3

The Spirit of God moved, hovered, or brooded upon the waters of this water-planet. The Hebrew words can be read as "a mighty wind," but that reading appeals most to those who deny the Creation and least to the harmony and unity of the Scriptures. The Creation in Genesis 1 is Trinitarian, just as the entire Bible is Trinitarian. One of the chief attributes of God throughout the Old Testament is Creator, whether we are reading Isaiah or Psalms. Although the nature of the Holy Trinity was not completely revealed until the time of Jesus, the hallmarks of the Triune God are present throughout the Old Testament.

The Aaronic blessing repeats *The Lord* three times. That is an odd way for an ancient leader to speak of God. And yet this was God's command to bless the children of Israel.

The LORD bless thee, and keep thee: The LORD make his face shine upon thee, and be gracious unto thee: The LORD lift up his countenance upon thee, and give thee peace. Numbers 6:24-26

This three-fold blessing remains the primary ending of our liturgical service.

Since God commanded that His name be three-fold, we can see that His intention was to reveal the Triune nature of the One God in time. During the First Day, the Three Persons participate in the Creation, for the Son of God is the creating Word, the command of God.

And God said means "through the Creating Word, the Son of God." The disciple closest to Jesus, John, revealed this his Creation Hymn:

In the beginning was the Word, and the Word was with God, and the Word was God. 2 The same was in the beginning with God. John 1:1

Only two books in the Bible have the same opening, which gives Genesis 1 and John 1 a unique bond, each one explaining the other, each one dependent upon the other. We cannot read the two Creation accounts apart from each other. John presupposes the Creation of Genesis while the first book of the Bible looks forward to the fulfillment of Creation in the redemption earned by the Creating Word, God incarnate.

If anyone is in doubt about the Son of God being the creating Word, another verses repeats the doctrine in another form.

He was in the world, and the world was made by him, and the world knew him not. John 1:10

God created light first, separating light from darkness. Like every aspect of Creation, this far surpasses our ability to comprehend. We think of light and darkness being governed by the sun and moon, or at least by power and power outages. However, the creation of light preceded the fashioning of the sun, moon, stars, and planets.

Evening and morning made up the first 24-hour day. Ancient and modern skeptics have stumbled over this time period. They do not like 24-hour days, but this is the only possible meaning of the Hebrew word for day. One Yale professor was called Old Yom because he insisted the Hebrew word *yom* could only include 24 hours. The term does not mean an era or epoch, as he proved from the text. The great minds of the 19th century wanted to lengthen the days to form a coalition with the Darwinists and evolution. They would allow for millions if not billions of years for Creation along the lines of evolution, giving God the slight honor for being extraordinarily slow in His work. This line of reasoning helped them feel safe among liberals, modernists, and others who shared their weak and sentimental attachment to the Bible.

This Munich Pact with the evolutionists did not keep the peace, showing how ardently people feel they must campaign against Genesis 1 and John 1. Any university scientist suspected of believing in Creation today is silenced, denied tenure, fired, or excommunicated in other ways, subtle or not. The issue is not so much the time element but Creation through the efficacy of the Word. Stretching out the time is another way of denying the power of God's Word to accomplish His will. Undermining Creation has been effective in weakening the foundation of our faith and the legal precepts of our country. Either God created or He did not. The Creation is divine only when divinely accomplished, not when reduced to man's understanding his science *du jour*.

Chaos Versus Order

People recognize that the natural state of man's world is chaos. If things do not begin in chaos, they quickly degenerate into chaos. For example, a home abandoned will have its windows broken and its furnishings trashed, its walls crumbling and its roof leaking. When we look at an abandoned house in a former ghost town like Jerome, Arizona, we think about the families that once lived there and then moved on after economic misfortunes.

Even occupied homes are in a constant state of breakdown and wear. Dirt accumulates. Appliances fail. Clothes and odd items accumulate in a jumble at an alarming rate. The surest sign of a chaotic mind is a home where tons of rubbish accumulates amid stacks of old papers and the filth of animals.

Someone's office, the scene of daily work, is also a filter catching every kind of rubbish, from old and current mail to scraps of food, paper, and books. Items defy identification, when the desk drawers are searched. Anonymous keys sit at the bottom of the drawer. Two padlocks, but the keys do not fit. There are some keys and they must be there for a reason. Here are batteries. They may be good or useless, so they are kept just in case they are needed. But there are only three AA batteries when four are required. One marker is dry. The other one is slowly leaking onto the liner paper. The permanent marker is grabbed to use on the erasable board at school. Three white boards are now tattooed with permanent black ink.

When people meet or try to govern any institution, conflict and confusion rule, even when rules are established for orderly business. Even with constitutions, Roberts Rules, and written statements of policies, people consume time and energy getting the least amount done. To solve the problem some assume dictatorial powers and rebellion breaks out, making matters worse than an autocrat could manage with the worst decisions.

In contrast, God's world is perfectly ordered, from the smallest detail to the largest. Man cannot perfect anything, but God's order is exquisitely detailed. When we look at man's handiwork under a scanning electron microscope, the finest craftsmanship betrays its flaws. The Swiss watch no longer looks so expensive. The gears appear misshapen and unbalanced, good enough for man but not up to God's standards. Every microscopic feature of an organism is a work of art in comparison. Red blood cells look like velvet pillows floating by. The focusing mechanism of the eye is maze of graceful lines, pulling and relaxing instantly and without effort. Cells betray greater complexity as we draw closer to their secrets, which man is trying to imitate in nanotechnology, an effort to create pumps, computers, and switches as tiny as those we take for granted in our own bodies.

The Right Order

Making coffee is a good example of the need for order. To make a pot, several steps must be taken or the enterprise will be a failure.

1. The coffee maker must be plugged in.
2. The water tank must be filled.
3. The coffee basket must contain fresh coffee grounds.
4. The start button must be pushed.
5. The opaque container must be emptied in advance.
6. The container must be put in the right position for proper flow of coffee.

Sometimes the coffee grounds are forgotten, yielding a pot of fresh, hot water. Sometimes the water is forgotten, so the machine hisses in imitation of making a pot while turning itself off in frustration, due to the temperature override. If the plug is forgotten, nothing happens. If everything is done right and the pot is half-full, the fresh coffee pours all over the counter. If the coffee grounds basket does not catch right, the coffee also pours all over the counter. Once the coffee pot was empty and the counter was clean, in spite of taking all the necessary steps except #6. The dry counter remained a surprise until the roll of paper towels revealed a brown color, a soggy nature, and the aroma of fresh coffee.

A Question of Purpose

The question of purpose has captivated people for countless ages. In modern times, Viktor Frankl, a survivor of Nazi work camps wrote *Man's Search for Meaning*, which is still a popular book, appreciated as much by college students now as it was 30 or more years ago. The very existence of a soul in every human being raises that question – what is man's purpose?

The study of God's creation raises the same question, but many times over, millions of times over. Even from the perspective of secular, non-religious study, no one has found a single item on this earth that does not have a purpose. Even the forces our weather systems have a purpose for the entire range of life. The snow covering the northern states protects far more than it harms. The interlocking crystals form the lightest possible blanket over the soil and plants, protecting from the desiccating winds of winter. Beneath the snow are myriads of dependent creatures that need the warming blanket to keep them through the coldest nights and days. When they create pockets and tunnels in the snow, comfortable bedrooms and living rooms are formed, with gentle blue light streaming in above. Although many animals and plants become dormant, they do not cease to function. The Eskimo copy their wisdom and thrive in the worst climate of all, fed by those animals designed to match their fortitude in winter.

A snowy winter in the northern states is a prelude for a riotous spring, when all the plants and animals emerge to bud, flourish, feed, and reproduce. One feeds upon another. One lives for the other. The predator becomes the prey in endless cycles while solemn morticians take away the dead, as ants do, or sanitize the place of death, as all carrion creatures do, from the crow to the maggot. Scientists marvel at this interlocking infinity of dependencies but they cannot answer the purpose. They can only describe what they see.

Each believer in Creation – even in the varied and strange religions of the world – understands that these dependencies are all the foundation of life for man, that they exist for man and require man's care. When man shows his gratitude for Creation, he is well fed and sheltered. When he destroys the complexities of life or tries to defy the laws established at the beginning of time, he is destroyed, not by God but by himself.

In contrast to the snowy winters of the North, we have those regions where little rain, no snow, and too much sun may be found. In a desert valley, the scientists marvel that the cacti thrive on neglect by wearing a coat of wax on their skin, storing water above ground in their flesh, and waiting patiently for a few inches of rain each year. If a saguaro cactus (the familiar one with arms) gets infected with insects, birds will peck them out of the flesh. The saguaro needs this pest patrol just as much as the birds need the food. However, the saguaro shows its gratitude by building a wooden-shoe in the hollow where the hole was carved during feeding. Birds then take up lodging in this birdhouse and continue their work of protecting their home and enlarging their real estate.

People look at the desert as barren, remembering the sand dunes of Yuma, Arizona in *Star Wars IV* or the shifting sands of the Empty Quarter in *Lawrence of Arabia*. When church members built their home on the northern edge of Phoenix, near vacant land, a visitor from St. Louis commented on how perfectly landscaped the vacant lot was. The empty land was covered with an attractive array of desert plants, spaced so evenly that a landscape architect seemed to be involved from the beginning.

Scientists say that the animals and plants of the desert adapted to their harsh climate, without explaining how these creatures first planned and then executed the changes necessary for their new home. Midwesterners throw away their woolen coats and their galoshes, drink more water, and buy sun blocker when they move to a desert. Did plants have a parlay before their trek and say, "We have to move to the desert, so we are going to produce skin wax and thorns"? Did the birds join a temperance league and forswear worms while changing their diets to insects?

The more we see the intricate chain of life on this earth, the more we understand how God has a purpose for each and every person. Although the weather, plants, and animals continue to serve their united purpose with a singular will, a divine will, man has the freedom to deny the purpose, reject any notion of a purpose, and live without serving anyone except himself. When a famous actor was asked whether his crippling accident had a higher purpose, he said, "No, it was just an accident."

If we look at the lives of those writers whose work delights children and adults, we find that they had the most miserable childhoods or painful adult experiences. Rudyard Kipling was treated savagely as he grew up, put in special institutions for the children of people serving in India. Beating was a common form of discipline in those horrible dens of self-righteousness, but Kipling grew up to write children's stories we still love, from *The Jungle Book* to his *Just So Stories*. Hans Christian Anderson suffered in different ways but excelled everyone in his fabulous stories, so numerous that my two-volume collection is the size of two huge Bibles. E. Nesbit was treated like a dog by her husband but her stories are filled with delight and humor. Nesbit is so famous in England that professional writers make a point of reading her stories over again each year.

Samuel Johnson is one of the most quoted writers of the English language. His father's bankruptcy forced Samuel out of Oxford, where he was an exceptional student. Johnson was afflicted with poor eyesight, a neurological condition, and bouts of crippling depression. The world of English literature forgets that he was a Christian, but people can judge for themselves from the prayer he wrote in his journal:

O Lord, who wouldst that all men should be saved, and who Knowest that without thy grace we can do nothing acceptable to thee, have mercy upon me. Enable me to break the chain of my sins, to reject sensuality in word and thought, and to overcome and suppress vain scruples; and to use such diligence in lawful employment as may enable me to support myself and do good to others. O Lord, forgive me the time lost in idleness; pardon the sins which I have committed, and grant that I may redeem the time misspent, and be reconciled to thee by true repentance, that I may live and die in peace, and be received to everlasting happiness. Take not from me, O Lord, thy Holy Spirit, but let me have support and comfort for Jesus Christ's sake. Amen.

Just as plants, animals, and the weather are linked together in an endless chain of dependencies, so are we humans, as often as we try to break that chain and form a new and man-centered one. People rush into all kinds of folly searching for that certitude they found so tedious in the Christian faith. Their mad pursuit of eco-religion, meditation, and paganism reflect the simple words of Augustine, the greatest orator of the Roman Empire , the most famous pagan of his time, the rebellious son who seemed immune to the prayers of his Christian mother Monica. In his *Confessions* , Augustine wrote:

"Thou hast made us for Thyself, and our hearts are restless until they rest in Thee."

The Second Day

And God said, Let there be a firmament in the midst of the waters, and let it divide the waters from the waters. 7 And God made the firmament, and divided the waters which *were* under the firmament from the waters which *were* above the firmament: and it was so. 8 And God called the firmament Heaven. And the evening and the morning were the second day. Genesis 1:6-7

The firmament refers to the vast expanse of the sky. Many have scoffed at the term, getting their meaning for firmament from the concept of the hammered out bowl. The Bible has many self-appointed editors who would love to improve the language of the Holy Spirit rather than deepen their understanding of the text. The bowl concept is not entirely wrong, since the earth's atmosphere is solid compared to the near-vacuum of space. When our vehicles return to the atmosphere they become fiery comets, glowing red with the friction of hitting the air particles at high speeds. The Space Shuttle requires a complicated system of tiles to keep this heat away from the metal ship and the passengers inside.

This firmament stretches out to protect all the inhabitants of earth from the direct radiation of the sun. We now realize more than ever how much the firmament is a shield against radiation hazards. This firmament must have changed over time. At first, a mist watered the earth (Genesis 2:6). After the Flood, seasons adjusted the heat and water cycles of the earth. Before the Flood, the entire earth was a blessed with remarkable abundance and balmy weather, as the geologic evidences shows. Therefore, the firmament was a misty shield of protection, a vast source of fresh water and fertility for the earth. Although we often forget this, our earth is 70% water and 30% land. God lifted the land out of the water.

For this they willingly are ignorant of, that by the word of God the heavens were of old, and the earth standing out of the water and in the water: 2 Peter 3:5

The watery chaos returned with the Flood and still creates terror and uncertainty today. The threat of flooding brought about the majestic Hoover Dam, but that was not enough. The City of Phoenix, in a desert valley, has a complex system of flood control to keep flash floods from destroying the economy.

Water-World

All life on earth is just as watery as its host. Our babies are born with 70% water content, just like Mother Earth, but children dry out in time. Adults are 50-60% water. Our need for water to sustain life is so great that the law requires Phoenix residents to give water to anyone who comes to the door and asks.

Our food is mostly water, but we consume more water in addition to our food. Pure water has become an upscale luxury, reminding people of the many lessons about water in the Bible.

When Jesus gave His lessons about water, near the water, or upon the water, He was teaching about the most basic element of life, an element He created. This should always guide our thoughts about the Gospel, that we are receiving this wisdom from Jesus as Lord and Creator.

Civilizations have grown up around water. The greatest cities in the world have been communities built near the sea, for food and commerce: Athens, Rome, Constantinople, London, and New York City. The Roman Empire made a science out of constructing aqueducts, heated baths, and water-heated homes.

Water into Wine

And the third day there was a marriage in Cana of Galilee; and the mother of Jesus was there: 2 And both Jesus was called, and his disciples, to the marriage. 3 And when they wanted wine, the mother of Jesus saith unto him, They have no wine. 4 Jesus saith unto her, Woman, what have I to do with thee? mine hour is not yet come. 5 His mother saith unto the servants, Whatsoever he saith unto you, do it. 6 And there were set there six waterpots of stone, after the manner of the purifying of the Jews, containing two or three firkins apiece. 7 Jesus saith unto them, Fill the waterpots with water. And they filled them up to the brim. 8 And he saith unto them, Draw out now, and bear unto the governor of the feast. And they bare it. 9 When the ruler of the feast had tasted the water that was made wine, and knew not whence it was: (but the servants which drew the water knew;) the governor of the feast called the bridegroom, 10 And saith unto him, Every man at the beginning doth set forth good wine; and when men have well drunk, then that which is worse: but thou hast kept the good wine until now. 11 This beginning of miracles did Jesus in Cana of Galilee, and manifested forth his glory; and his disciples believed on him. John 2:1-11

In this Gospel we have a miracle that is so remarkable that it made the divinity of Christ apparent to everyone. People have always claimed to have the power to heal others. We often hear the claim today. Some fakes use animal parts and pretend to pull them out of their patients through "psychic surgery." Pentecostal healers carefully select those whose ailments can improve temporarily with a shift in mood. Arthritis and hearing problems are quite variable, so an instant cure seems impressive. One fake named Popof was exposed for using a radio setup with his wife. She sent him messages in his earphone about personal information on the cards of members in the audience. So Rev. Popof could miraculously tell someone that her sister was ill, or that she had a son named Bob. Once he displayed his amazing powers, thanks to the hidden microphone, Popof could fool the audience about anything. As I said, Popof was exposed a few years ago, disgraced, and now he is back again on television. Televangelists are an inspiration to any politician in trouble.

But with this miracle the claim is very clear. The people knew they were out of wine. The servants knew they were dealing with water. They filled the water pots with water. If they had poured in wine by mistake or through cunning, the aroma would have given them away. The texture of wine is also quite different. I doubt whether the whitest wine could pass for water, especially in a culture where wine was a daily staple.

At the Word of Jesus, the water became wine. No one asked for a miracle or looked for a miracle, except Mary. Mary knew her Son had the ability to solve the problem. Most mothers think so, but in this text we can see that she is asking for something beyond His immediate desire to fulfill. His response is at least a mild rebuke.

Here the translators often think they are wiser than the Holy Spirit. They do not like Jesus calling His mother woman, so they add words, softening *woman* (the actual text) to *dear woman* (more appealing but inaccurate).

"Dear woman, why do you involve me?" Jesus replied. "My time has not yet come. John 2:4 (NIV)

Twice when Jesus addressed His mother directly in the Gospel of John, He called her woman instead of "mother." This shows us that He was her Lord and not just a son.

The proper role of Mary is seen in the Scriptures as the mother of Jesus who raised Him in faith. She was a mortal woman, a sinner who died in the same way all must die. She did not fully understand her Son, as shown in the incident in the Temple, but she believed in Him and had a major role in the apostolic church. She is named early in Acts and then never again. (We should marvel that the apostles did not make a cult out of Mary then, for she was there at the beginning and had many years of memories of Him. So we see that the apostles resisted the urge to concentrate on Mary. Instead they preached the Gospel of Christ.)

This miracle raises the issue of justifying faith.

This beginning of miracles did Jesus in Cana of Galilee, and manifested forth his glory; and his disciples believed on him. John 2:11

When we speak about faith, the word faith can have many meanings.

1. For instance, everyone has faith or trust in something. The atheist Carl Sagen did not believe in God, but he believed in extraterrestrials. He needed to. Anyone who insists on evolution must have life on other planets, to prove that life can generate itself spontaneously, without God being involved.

2. The epistle of James speaks about dead faith. Lutherans should not be afraid of this letter or fail to study it. The Gospel always brings the fruit of the Spirit. If the fruit is lacking, then it points to a lack of faith. We see that in many church leaders who can speak the right words but keep themselves in power through lies, slander, and protecting false teachers. It is good to remember their faith and avoid falling into the same trap. As James says

quite vividly, "The demons believe and their hides bristle." That is not justifying faith. It is an awareness of the power of the Word: hating and fearing it.

3. Faith in miracles. Martin Chemnitz writes about this in his Loci, and it should make us think. Many hundreds if not thousands saw the miracles of Jesus. Certainly this happened at the wedding feast, at the grave of Lazarus, and in many other instances. They believed it was a miracle but they did not necessarily follow Jesus or believe in Him as their Savior.

4. Historical faith. Many scholars and people on the perimeter of Christianity have faith in the basic facts about the Bible. They even believe in the historical truth of the Bible. But it never goes farther than that. Luther said in many ways that it does no good to say that Christ died for the sins of the world if we fail to say, "and for me." Unless we say, Christ died for my sins, we only have historical faith.

5. *Kohlerglaube* . A collier's faith is based upon an incident where a coal handler was asked what he believed. "I believe what the church believes." And what does the church believe? "The church believes what I believe." In other words, it is just an attachment to the institution, without knowing much or believing. Although this can bring a whole family or ethnic group to church, it is easy for someone to hear the Word and reject it by saying, "This is the right place. All my friends and relatives are here."

This shows how many ways faith can be something other than justifying faith.
Chemnitz and the authors of the Book of Concord were anxious to teach the proper understanding of faith.

But when we are speaking of the subject itself, it is certain that the doctrine of gracious reconciliation, of the remission of sins, of righteousness, salvation, and eternal life through faith for the sake of the Mediator is one and the same in the Old and in the New Testament. This is a useful rule which we must retain at all costs: The doctrine, wherever we read it, in either the Old or New Testament, which deals with the gracious reconciliation and the remission of sins through faith for the sake of God's mercy in Christ, is the Gospel." (Chemnitz, 1989, *Loci Theologici* , II, p. 459)

This is beautifully expressed by Melanchthon, the primary author of the Augsburg Confession:

Thus when we say that we are justified by faith, we are saying nothing else than that for the sake of the Son of God we receive remission of sins and are accounted as righteous. And because it is necessary that this benefit be taken hold of, this is said to be done 'by faith,' that is, by trust in the mercy promised us for the sake of Christ. Thus we must also understand the correlative expression, 'We are righteous by faith,' that is, through the mercy of God for the sake of His Son we are righteous or accepted. (Melanchthon, Loci Communes, "The Word Faith." Cited in Martin Chemnitz, *Loci Theologici*, II, p. p. 489.)

Lutherans confess in the Book of Concord, in harmony with Luther, that we are justified by faith alone:

For neither you nor I could ever know anything of Christ, or believe on Him, and obtain Him for our Lord, unless it were offered to us and granted to our hearts by the Holy Ghost through the preaching of the Gospel. The work is done and accomplished; for Christ has acquired and gained the treasure for us by His suffering, death, resurrection, etc. But if the work remained concealed so that no one knew of it, then it would be in vain and lost. That this treasure, therefore, might not lie buried, but be appropriated and enjoyed, God has caused the Word to go forth and be proclaimed, in which He gives the Holy Ghost to bring this treasure home and appropriate it to us. Therefore sanctifying is nothing else than bringing us to Christ to receive this good, to which could not attain of ourselves. (The Large Catechism, The Creed, Article III, #38, *Concordia Triglotta*, St. Louis: Concordia Publishing House, 1921, p. 689. Tappert, p. 415.)

The Vine

And when he was entered into a ship, his disciples followed him. 24 And, behold, there arose a great tempest in the sea, insomuch that the ship was covered with the waves: but he was asleep. 25 And his disciples came to him, and awoke him, saying, Lord, save us: we perish. 26 And he saith unto them, Why are ye fearful, O ye of little faith? Then he arose, and rebuked the winds and the sea; and there was a great calm. 27 But the men marvelled, saying, What manner of man is this, that even the winds and the sea obey him! Matthew 8:23-27

Ye of Little Faith

In this Gospel we have a brief but powerful lesson about faith and lack of faith.

The foundation for many different errors is confusion about the two natures of Christ. Jesus was and is both divine and human, God and man. Before the Holy Spirit conceived the child in the Virgin Mary, the Son of God existed from all eternity, but only in His divine nature. From the moment of conception the Son of God took on our human nature without losing any of His divine nature. He has both natures now. In that respect the Holy Trinity changed in time, since the Word of God became Incarnate in the Virgin Mary.

This is important to remember when we read the text about the stilling of the storm. Travel by foot or by donkey was slow and arduous in Palestine. Those who live in the desert can easily imagine why anyone would travel in a boat straight across a lake rather than walk around it. The Sea of Galilee is not a gentle fishing lake, but a large body of water, easily tossed about by storms and great winds.

The cults do not realize this, but Jesus chose to hide His divine nature most of the time. It was never absent, but it was often difficult to imagine that this ordinary looking man was anything other than a teacher. The disciples saw many displays of God's power in Jesus and yet they still forgot.

We should not be quick to condemn them for being block-heads. We know far more than they could imagine. We can look back at the miraculous spread of Christianity, at the glorious lives of the apostles, the unfolding of church history. Centuries of sincere believers have explained the Biblical texts to us. And yet we doubt.

And how do we doubt? We doubt when we are in exactly the same position as the disciples. In the midst of a great storm that seems to overwhelm us, we stop viewing our world with faith and start looking at the raw facts. No one can really do that. We process the facts with our minds. We start filtering. Our emotions take over. And they are remarkable filters.

Have you ever been afraid in the dark? Any sound or movement can make you jump and suck in your breath. Sweat breaks out, even in cold weather. Hands get moist. One fact after another increases the fear. The sounds and the movements are raw facts, but the fearful mind turns them into terrifying evidence. My wife Chris and I were walking down the street in downtown Chicago, late at night. We heard steps behind us. We walked faster. The steps quickened. We looked at each other. We were being stalked. We were sure of that. Downtown Chicago. Late at night. No police in sight. We could hear the steps getting closer. I decided to look at our assailant, perhaps to have some evidence to offer, this side of the morgue. I saw a somewhat familiar face. "Jack?" It was Jack Preus, president of the LCMS. He was walking back to the same hotel, for the LCA convention, 1978. Fear vanished. He said, "Are you one of ours?" I said, "No." Years later he signed my copy of *The Two Natures of Christ*, by Martin Chemnitz, and we discussed a few things.

Luther reminds us that fear and faith are opposites. The lack of faith causes fear. Fear leads to despair. Many people live in despair even though their outward circumstances are pleasant and stable. The facts do not mean much. In fact, telling someone not to worry because of the facts is rather fruitless. It's like yelling shut-up at a crying baby. It relieves tension in the speaker but not in the listener.

The disciples were frantic in the storm. The waves were swamping the boat, which was large and flat-bottomed, to provide stability in those waters. All of us would have been scared, too. Jesus was asleep. Looking at this from our perspective, we can say, "If the King of Creation is asleep in my boat, then I am not going to worry."

But at that moment they did not see the Lord of Creation but their beloved teacher, a man, asleep. They saw indifference.

And he was in the hinder part of the ship, asleep on a pillow: and they awake him, and say unto him, Master, carest thou not that we perish? Mark 4:38

Once again, we can place ourselves in that same boat. How often has each one of us said, in one way or another, "Lord, don't you care that I am suffering?" Although hundreds of passages in the Bible tell us that God does care, that Jesus does understand our fears and weakness, we still fall into the same frame of mind.

God knows that our doubts make us fearful. He tells us not to be afraid, but He teaches us why we should not be fearful and anxious. The antidote to doubt, anxiety, and fear is the Gospel promise. The more we hear the promises of God, the more confidence we have in Him. "I believe, Lord. Help thou mine unbelief."

And straightway the father of the child cried out, and said with tears, Lord, I believe; help thou mine unbelief. Mark 9:24

Do Not Be Afraid

After these things the word of the LORD came unto Abram in a vision, saying, Fear not, Abram: I am thy shield, and thy exceeding great reward. Genesis 15:1

And he said, I am God, the God of thy father: fear not to go down into Egypt; for I will there make of thee a great nation: Genesis 46:3

The LORD is on my side; I will not fear: what can man do unto me? Psalm 118:6

Fear thou not; for I am with thee: be not dismayed; for I am thy God: I will strengthen thee; yea, I will help thee; yea, I will uphold thee with the right hand of my righteousness. Isaiah 41:10

Fear not, little flock; for it is your Father's good pleasure to give you the kingdom. Luke 12:32

For ye have not received the spirit of bondage again to fear; but ye have received the Spirit of adoption, whereby we cry, Abba, Father. Romans 8:15

For God hath not given us the spirit of fear; but of power, and of love, and of a sound mind. 2 Timothy 1:7

Be careful for nothing {do not be anxious}; but in every thing by prayer and supplication with thanksgiving let your requests be made known unto God. Philippians 4:6

Antidote to Fear

The antidote to fear is clearly revealed in the text. The disciples awakened Jesus by saying, "Save us, we are perishing." Notice what the little Gospel says, using that same verb, perish:

For God so loved the world, that he gave his only begotten Son, that whosoever believeth in him should not perish, but have everlasting life. John 3:16

Jesus berated the disciples for saying they were perishing when they were in the same boat with God Incarnate, God-in-the-Flesh (the literal meaning of God Incarnate). Although the disciples only saw the human nature of Jesus, His divine nature was not missing or inactive in any way. Jesus quickly rebuked the storm, silencing the wind and waves. Only God can perform such a miracle.

Why did Jesus allow the disciples to become so fearful before He revealed His awesome power? Times of great fear, despair, or anxiety show us how weak we really are. Then, when we see how God takes care of us through His Word, in an instant, we grow in faith.

This is extremely important. Faith either increases or shrinks away. God allows us to go through times of trial so that our trust in Him grows.

Lutherans have become terribly afraid of the word faith. I do not know exactly why. It is the most frequent word in the Bible and the Book of Concord. The word *faith* appears in the KJV 247 times, without counting the verb (*believe*) or such compounds as *faithful* and *little-faith* . When faith grows in an individual, it is solely because of the effect of the Word. In other words, faith grows when the believer knows and believes what God is like and what God can do.

Our daily experiences create a little school where we receive our lessons. Too many people, especially in the secular world, think that the experience itself is good. But it is God's Word informing us about our role in His kingdom, and experience opens our eyes to what God can do and what we cannot do. The more we grow in faith, the more we have confidence in God and lose confidence in ourselves. I know that will not sell on TV talk shows, but it is the essence of the Christian faith.

We are by nature self-centered and prone to imagine we have the answers. The Christian faith takes our attention away from ourselves and turns our eyes toward God, what He has done and what He will do.
In this light the most important storm God can quell with His Word is the turbulence caused by sin.

Therefore being justified by faith, we have peace with God through our Lord Jesus Christ: 2 By whom also we have access by faith into this grace wherein we stand, and rejoice in hope of the glory of God. Romans 5:1-2

Forgiveness gives us peace with God. Jesus gives us forgiveness through His cross. The Gospel says to us: This is your faith, Christ crucified for your sins. He has paid the price. Gone are the illusions that we can atone for our sins. Vanished are all the promises that we can improve ourselves by our own willpower. The broken bones rejoice (Psalm 51) because the Gospel brings healing, comfort, peace, joy, and genuine love.

Romantic love is a wonderful thing. God blesses the love of a husband and wife with children. To love a child is one of the greatest blessings of this world. At the art museum in Phoenix we ran into a woman who adopted a child, her only child, at the age of 50. On the way to the museum we were talking about how children bless us by taking away our self-centeredness. This woman with her adopted girl from Korea seemed to be a young mother because she was filled with such delight and wonder at this little creature now given to her. The little girl was shunned and pointed at in Korea for being half-American. She was just 19 months old. Now she was being touched and complimented. After a long conversation, she smiled and blew kisses.

This is what God does to us. As sinners we deserve nothing more than condemnation, being shunned by the Almighty. But because we are justified by faith, God treats us as beloved, as the prophet Isaiah teaches us:

Thou shalt also be a crown of glory in the hand of the LORD, and a royal diadem in the hand of thy God. 4 Thou shalt no more be termed Forsaken; neither shall thy land any more be termed Desolate: but thou shalt be called Hephzibah, and thy land Beulah: for the LORD delighteth in thee, and thy land shall be married. 5 For as a young man marrieth a virgin, so shall thy sons marry thee: and as the bridegroom rejoiceth over the bride, so shall thy God rejoice over thee. Isaiah 62:3-5

God rejoices over us because Christ has made us part of His flock. Being loved by God bears fruit in our lives as sinners forgiven, justified by faith.

The Tree of Life

The Third Day

And God said, Let the waters under the heaven be gathered together unto one place, and let the dry *land* appear: and it was so. 10 And God called the dry *land* Earth; and the gathering together of the waters called he Seas: and God saw that *it was* good. 11 And God said, Let the earth bring forth grass, the herb yielding seed, *and* the fruit tree yielding fruit after his kind, whose seed *is* in itself, upon the earth: and it was so. 12 And the earth brought forth grass, *and* herb yielding seed after his kind, and the tree yielding fruit, whose seed *was* in itself, after his kind: and God saw that *it was* good. 13 And the evening and the morning were the third day. Genesis 1:9-12

No statement has summarized the lessons of this Day of Creation better than the following:

Now, although both, the planting and watering of the preacher, and the running and willing of the hearer, would be in vain, and no conversion would follow it if the power and efficacy of the Holy Ghost were not added thereto, who enlightens and converts the hearts through the Word preached and heard, so that men believe this Word and assent thereto, still, neither preacher nor hearer is to doubt this grace and efficacy of the Holy Ghost, but should be certain that when the Word of God is preached purely and truly, according to the command and will of God, and men listen attentively and earnestly and meditate upon it, God is certainly present with His grace, and grants, as has been said, what otherwise man can neither accept nor give from his own powers. (Solid Declaration, Article II, Free Will, 55-56, Formula of Concord , *Concordia Triglotta* , p. 903. Tappert, p. 531f.)

The Herb Yielding Seed

Every seed is alive, created to seek every possible opportunity to germinate and grow. Some weed seeds can remain dormant for decades, waiting for the soil to turn over and generate the warmth for needed for growth. Moisture is often the key ingredient, so children love to place seeds in moist paper towels and watch the life of the seeds erupt into pale seedlings.

Soil and plants are created for each other. Most of the nutrition for all plants, trees included, is exchanged in the top 12 inches of soil. The roots hold the soil and the soil feeds the roots. The complexity of this system alone is enough to fill several textbooks.

When Jesus spoke of the seed as the Word, He gave us a comparison so vivid that no one should forget.

And when much people were gathered together, and were come to him out of every city, he spake by a parable: 5 A sower went out to sow his seed: and as he sowed, some fell by the way side; and it was trodden down, and the fowls of the air devoured it. 6 And some fell upon a rock; and as soon as it was sprung up, it withered away, because it lacked moisture. 7 And some fell among thorns; and the thorns sprang up with it, and choked it. 8 And other fell on good ground, and sprang up, and bare fruit an hundredfold. And when he had said these things, he cried, He that hath ears to hear, let him

hear. **9 And his disciples asked him, saying, What might this parable be? 10 And he said, Unto you it is given to know the mysteries of the kingdom of God: but to others in parables; that seeing they might not see, and hearing they might not understand. 11 Now the parable is this: The seed is the word of God. 12 Those by the way side are they that hear; then cometh the devil, and taketh away the word out of their hearts, lest they should believe and be saved. 13 They on the rock *are they*, which, when they hear, receive the word with joy; and these have no root, which for a while believe, and in time of temptation fall away. 14 And that which fell among thorns are they, which, when they have heard, go forth, and are choked with cares and riches and pleasures of *this* life, and bring no fruit to perfection. 15 But that on the good ground are they, which in an honest and good heart, having heard the word, keep *it*, and bring forth fruit with patience. Luke 8:4-15**

This is one of the central texts in the Bible about the efficacy of the Word, answering why the Gospel is proclaimed and yet many do not believe in the Promises of God.

One of the problems people find in this text is the statement about teaching the Word so that people see without seeing and hear without understanding. And yet it is also clear that the parables are taught so that the lessons are easy to remember.

Faith in Christ is a gift of the Holy Spirit. Without faith the parables are nice stories that mean nothing in particular. Many examples can be found of this kind of interpretation. For instance, people write about the Bible as literature or as history. The Scriptures are historical and they are literature but without faith they have very little meaning. One liberal New Testament professor in seminary wrote and published a book on the parables of Jesus. However, he did not believe the basic articles of the Christian faith and often made fun of them. He scoffed at the resurrection accounts of the Gospels. He listened without hearing, saw without perceiving, and had no faith.

The Scriptures are nothing to people without faith. Christ appointed apostles and established the ministry so that the Gospel would be proclaimed, taught, and administered by those with proper training. Notice how quickly the apostates seek out seminary professorships. They want others to be exactly like them. Normally faith comes to people through the spoken or external Word. Luther used the term "external word" to distinguish it from the Pentecostal types who said they listened to the internal voice of God. Although a few people are converted simply by reading the Scriptures, the vast majority of people come to faith through the spoken Word. That includes Holy Baptism, where the spoken Word united with water converts the child.

So if someone has not been converted, hearing the parables is not very illuminating. Nevertheless, even the coarsest person can remember the basic details of this great parable and ask about the meaning of it. Jesus explained it to His disciples and they passed on the teaching ministry to pastors. One way the parables have their effect is to allow people to study them in detail through the teaching ministry of the pastor.

Anyone can understand the Scriptures, but it is also true that people left to themselves will invent almost anything about the Bible. The same heresies keep being repeated because people make up whatever they want and turn that into their religion. Laity and pastors fall into these errors. That is why we have conferences to discuss doctrine, to clarify and confess what we believe.

The parable of the Sower and the Seed is easy to remember because the details are so close to what we know from gardening. The seed is the Word of God. The types of soil represents where it falls when it is broadcast. (Liberals complain about figurative language in the Scriptures. Did you ever think that our term for TV and radio is really a metaphor for sowing seed? – broadcasting) There are four categories. That does not mean that each one represents 25%. We know from our own experience that in sowing seed "some" may be any number.

Hardened Footpath

Some seed falls on the hardened footpath and is snatched up by the birds and devoured. The lost seed are those who had faith but lost it and remain within the visible church. They are the apostates who rule the visible church today.

The first class of disciples are those who hear the Word but neither understand nor esteem it. And these are not the mean people of the world, but the greatest, wisest and the most saintly, in short they are the greatest part of mankind; for Christ does not speak here of those who persecute the Word nor of those who fail to give their ear to it, but of those who hear it and are students of it, who also wish to be called true Christian and to live in Christian fellowship with Christians and are partakers of baptism and the Lord's Supper. But they are of a carnal heart, and remain so, failing to appropriate the Word of God to themselves, it goes in one ear and out the other, just like the seed along the wayside did not fall into the earth, but remained lying on the ground...(Sermons *of Martin Luther*, II, p. 114.)

Rocky Ground

Some seed falls on rocky ground. It springs up quickly and then withers in the heat of the day. The withered plants are those who receive faith from the preaching of the Gospel, jump for joy, and then fall away when bad things happen to them. Many ministers find they must bear the cross instead of enjoying a secure and sedate life. Their initial joy turns into sorrow and they fall away. Many celebrity conversions are like this. Someone is terribly and horribly repentant at first and then realizes it is a lot more fun to be a hellion than an angel. Pentecostals often fall away because the initial rush they felt from the tongue-speaking experience could not be maintained.

The second class of hearers are those who receive the Word with joy, but they do not persevere. These are also a large multitude who understand the Word correctly and lay hold of it in its purity without any spirit of sect, division or fanaticism, they rejoice also in that they know the real truth, and are able to know how they may be saved without works through faith...But when the sun shines hot it withers, because it has no soil and moisture, and only rock is there. So these do; in times of persecution they deny or keep silence about the Word and work, speak and suffer all that their persecutors mention or wish, who formerly went forth and spoke, and confessed with a fresh and joyful spirit the same, while there was peace and no heat, so that there was hope they would bear much fruit and serve the people. (Sermons *of Martin Luther*, II, p. 116)

Among Thorns

Some seed falls among thorns. We have all seen plants like this. We notice a useful plant come up and then a weed nearby. We think, "I will get to that weed when I have a little more time." Suddenly the weed engulfs and overshadows the good plant. These people are the ones who have a good start and then let all kinds of concerns dwarf and devour their faith. Some find that Sundays are the best time for children's sports. Others want one morning a week free (and Saturday is now frantic day for many families). Still others get wrapped up in work, hobbies, or old-fashioned hedonism.

Therefore they [fallen among thorns] do not earnestly give themselves to the Word, but become indifferent and sink in the cares, riches and pleasures of this life, so that they are of no benefit to anyone. Therefore they are like the seed that fell among the thorns...They know their duty but do it not, they teach but do not practice what they teach, and are this year as they were last. (Sermons *of Martin Luther*, II, p. 117.)

Good Soil

Finally there is the good ground that produces fruit with patience over time. Gardeners complain about all the problems introduced by Adam and Eve, but the same growers also pass along bags of produce. Late summer always bring out the zuke passing, when people who love zucchini and even preserve zucchini find out nevertheless they cannot keep up with the vines, so they give away pounds of it. People warned us that if we planted two more lemon trees we would soon have enough for the City of Glendale.

Jesus' point in this parable is that the good ground will more than make up for the failures caused by man and Satan's temptations.

Luke 8:15 But that on the good ground are they, which in an honest and good heart, having heard the word, keep *it* , and bring forth fruit with patience.

There is so much in this verse that we should dwell on it and memorize it. What is an honest and good heart? A family of morticians divided themselves up among five different denominations to go to church. Some suspected that they did this to maximize their funeral business. Others have been known to switch from Lutheran to Presbyterian when their income got high enough for them to go high society and abandon their blue-collar group. This happened in Canada. When Lutherans got to a certain level of income, they joined the Presbyterian church across the street. One executive at Dow lost 20 pounds and joined the Presbyterian church – where the Dow family attended – in his quest for a better job.

Keeping the Word of God can be compared to guarding something precious. The word in the New Testament for *keeping* is also used for guarding a jail. When we have something special, we make sure nothing can take it away from us. We put jewels in a safe. We lock china in a display case. We put cigars in humidor.

Keeping the Word means guarding it in the same way we watch over material things that matter to us. However, the Word is far more important. The Word will always remain the Word, even if no one ever believes it, but it cannot be very precious to many people who either attack it or fashion it according to their self-centered ideas. Every day I see strange bumper stickers in the college parking lot proclaiming belief in the occult, same-sex marriages, and the like.

The Word brings forth fruit in time when we have patience. A valuable crop in the garden does not arrive overnight. No one expects a new fruit tree to bear right away. Asparagus is valued especially because we have to wait several years for the first crop. The slowest growing varieties of sweet corn are considered the best. Fast growing seed was available so farmers could keep their corn stands loaded during a long season, but the best white corn was the longest growing from start to finish – Silver Queen. And it was always worth the wait.

The Word brings forth fruit in our own lives and in future generations. If a couple sincerely believes in the Word and they raise their children to believe in the Gospel, they will eventually have dozens if not hundreds of believers in future generations.

This parable answers the question denominations have been asking (in vain) for decades. They have asked in vain because they wanted a material answer to a spiritual question. How can we make sure that the church will keep growing? The answer is simple, although exact predictions cannot be predicted or charted.

Imperishable Seed

Forasmuch as ye know that ye were not redeemed with corruptible things, *as* silver and gold, from your vain conversation *received* by tradition from your fathers; 19 But with the precious blood of Christ, as of a lamb without blemish and without spot: 20 Who verily was foreordained before the foundation of the world, but was manifest in these last times for you, 21 Who by him do believe in God, that raised him up from the dead, and gave him glory; that your faith and hope might be in God. 22 Seeing ye have purified your souls in obeying the truth through the Spirit unto unfeigned love of the brethren, *see that ye* love one another with a pure heart fervently: 23 Being born again, not of corruptible seed, but of incorruptible, by the word of God, which liveth and abideth for ever. 24 For all flesh *is* as grass, and all the glory of man as the flower of grass. The grass withereth, and the flower thereof falleth away: 25 But the word of the Lord endureth for ever. And this is the word which by the gospel is preached unto you. 1 Peter 1:18-25

To have a large crop, sow more seed. That is not difficult. Sow even more seed. Sow pure seed, not weed seed. Sing orthodox Lutheran hymns. Read orthodox Lutheran authors. Study a faithful translation of the Bible. Listen to faithful pastors and avoid the apostates. Publish orthodox Lutheran books, orthodox Lutheran websites, and orthodox Lutheran booklets. Sow the imperishable seed.

The preaching of this message may be likened to a stone thrown into the water, producing ripples which circle outward from it, the waves rolling always on and on, one driving the other, till they come to the shore. Although the center becomes quiet, the waves do not rest, but move forward. So it is with the preaching of the Word. It was begun by the apostles, and it constantly goes forward, is pushed on farther and farther by the preachers, driven hither and thither into the world, yet always being made known to those who never heard it before, although it be arrested in the midst of its course and is condemned as heresy. (Sermons *of Martin Luther*, III, p. 202)

The Fourth Day

And God said, Let there be lights in the firmament of the heaven to divide the day from the night; and let them be for signs, and for seasons, and for days, and years: 15 And let them be for lights in the firmament of the heaven to give light upon the earth: and it was so. 16 And God made two great lights; the greater light to rule the day, and the lesser light to rule the night: *he made* the stars also. 17 And God set them in the firmament of the heaven to give light upon the earth, 18 And to rule over the day and over the night, and to divide the light from the darkness: and God saw that *it was* good. 19 And the evening and the morning were the fourth day. Genesis 1:14-19

seasons

The Star of Bethlehem

Now when Jesus was born in Bethlehem of Judaea in the days of Herod the king, behold, there came wise men from the east to Jerusalem, 2 Saying, Where is he that is born King of the Jews? for we have seen his star in the east, and are come to worship him. 3 When Herod the king had heard *these things* , he was troubled, and all Jerusalem with him. 4 And when he had gathered all the chief priests and scribes of the people together, he demanded of them where Christ should be born. 5 And they said unto him, In Bethlehem of Judaea: for thus it is written by the prophet, 6 And thou Bethlehem , *in* the land of Juda , art not the least among the princes of Juda: for out of thee shall come a Governor, that shall rule my people Israel . 7 Then Herod, when he had privily called the wise men, enquired of them diligently what time the star appeared. 8 And he sent them to Bethlehem , and said, Go and search diligently for the young child; and when ye have found *him* , bring me word again, that I may come and worship him also. 9 When they had heard the king, they departed; and, lo, the star, which they saw in the east, went before them, till it came and stood over where the young child was. 10 When they saw the star, they rejoiced with exceeding great joy. 11 And when they were come into the house, they saw the young child with Mary his mother, and fell down, and worshipped him: and when they had opened their treasures, they presented unto him gifts; gold, and frankincense, and myrrh. 12 And being warned of God in a dream that they should not return to Herod, they departed into their own country another way. Matthew 2:1-12

Around 50 years ago, one of the certain proofs of Jesus being a myth was the Star of Bethlehem. Nothing made the apostates smirk more than the thought of a new star leading the Wise Men to the baby in Bethlehem. They thought this miracle was too convenient to be genuine, so they dismissed it as being invented.

One of the interesting things about searching the topic on the Internet is how many sites are devoted to ending belief in the Star of Bethlehem. One site even complained:

Every Christmas planetariums across the country present a *Star of Bethlehem* show, which breaks attendance records and balances their budget for the year. They are pandering to naive public fascination with the question, and generally trot out a whole parade of scenarios about astronomical events, which might have been the stimulus for the Biblical story.

The Naval Observatory lists a series of events, which could have been associated with the Star of Bethlehem.

The Navy essay raises the possibility that the Wise Men began to travel toward Bethlehem when the first astronomical events started in 7 BC. Although no one can say absolutely which stellar event was the Star of Bethlehem, we now have the happy result of much research, no longer denying the Star but wondering which phenomenon was the Star.

Truly hip theologians do not want to discuss the historical nature of Biblical stories, but such considerations are essential. Christianity is a religion where God is always part of history and enters history in the Incarnation. All our dates in the Western world are based upon the birth of Christ and that Star. One person made the interesting observation that a calendar is very much an expression of culture. There is a Jewish calendar with different dates and an Islamic calendar with another set of dates. Year zero means a lot for a culture.

Jesus, as the Creating Word, established the heavens and the earth. The eternal Son of God so arranged the vastness of space so that a series of unique events would herald His birth to the astronomers/astrologers of the East. While He was in his manger bed, the Wise Men were traveling toward Him, following His planets, which were wandering in His constellations of stars. The contrast between the baby and the stars He created remind me of the great Gerhard hymn (The *Lutheran Hymnal* 142):

> O Love, how strong Thou art to save!
>
> Thou beddest Him within the grave
>
> Whose Word the mountains rendeth.

We like to think of the ancient peoples as primitive, without our great scientific knowledge, but recent discoveries have shown that the Greeks could predict the movement of the planets and display it with a geared device, centuries before Christ. Archimedes invented the odometer, and we did not rediscover it until modern times. DaVinci could not reproduce it.

The ancients knew all about the motion of planets (planet, Greek for wanderer) against the tapestry of the stars. The constellations rose and set every evening, always in the same relationship to each other. The bright planets wandered around the stars, giving the ancients much to consider since each star and constellation had meaning for them. The intellectuals of many empires would have been curious about the meaning of the Star of Bethlehem. That men traveled to see the new king is a testimony to the attraction of the Star.

The meaning of the Star is even more important than its historical nature. The Star announced the Light of the World, as Isaiah teaches (the epistle for the Day of Epiphany):

Arise, shine; for thy light is come, and the glory of the LORD is risen upon thee. 2 For, behold, the darkness shall cover the earth, and gross darkness the people: but the LORD shall arise upon thee, and his glory shall be seen upon thee. 3 And the Gentiles shall come

to thy light, and kings to the brightness of thy rising. 4 Lift up thine eyes round about, and see: all they gather themselves together, they come to thee: thy sons shall come from far, and thy daughters shall be nursed at *thy* side. 5 Then thou shalt see, and flow together, and thine heart shall fear, and be enlarged; because the abundance of the sea shall be converted unto thee, the forces of the Gentiles shall come unto thee. 6 The multitude of camels shall cover thee, the dromedaries of Midian and Ephah; all they from Sheba shall come: they shall bring gold and incense; and they shall shew forth the praises of the LORD. Isaiah 60:1-6

As Luther wisely observes, the light is only meant to shine in darkness. If light already exists, there is no need for light. But when there is utter darkness, the light shines more brilliantly. The Gospel brings light to people because it conveys Christ and His benefits to those who receive Him in faith. The benefits are joy, unity, love, patience, and the peace that comes from being forgiven.

Note the contrast in Isaiah's lesson:

2 For, behold, the darkness shall cover the earth, and gross darkness the people: but the LORD shall arise upon thee, and his glory shall be seen upon thee. 3 And the Gentiles shall come to thy light, and kings to the brightness of thy rising.

There is only utter gross darkness on one side and light, glory, and brightness on the other. Just as the Bible knows only belief and unbelief, with no middle ground, so the Word of God only teaches light and darkness, with no intermediary light (of human reason).

The Bible is not revelation if man can already come to an understanding through his own reason. The natural man neither knows nor fears God.

But the natural man receiveth not the things of the Spirit of God: for they are foolishness unto him: neither can he know *them*, because they are spiritually discerned. 1 Corinthians 2:14

Those who try to make Christianity appealing to the scientific person, softening the edges of revelation, make a worse hash of matters than any pagan. The tendency in using reason the wrong way is to take away what seems foolish to the modern mind. The ancient mind was often superstitious, seeing many gods in various objects. The modern mind is secular, refusing to see God's power in the earthquake, wind, and tsunami. A video from the Weather Channel showed some young men caught in their car in a hailstorm where the hail was as big as baseballs, even larger. They ran for their lives and hid in a basement. The ancients would have reacted by sacrificing an animal or even a human. We explain weather fronts.

According to these self-appointed experts, Paul would have appealed to the ancients (using reason as an intermediary light) by agreeing with their superstitions. Today the same reasonable people would have the Apostle Paul demonstrate his abilities in sales. In both cases the true nature of God is pushed aside for what is popular for the moment. When Norman Vincent Peale was popular for reducing Christianity to success stories, one wit said, "I find Paul appealing and Peale appalling."

Instead of accommodating himself to the spirit of the times, Paul relied on God's Word to convert his listeners. He did not seek a compromise with man's wisdom but trusted instead in the folly of God's wisdom to make foolish the wisdom of the wise. There can only be truth and falsehood, light and darkness, faith and unbelief.

The night is far spent, the day is at hand: let us therefore cast off the works of darkness, and let us put on the armor of light. Romans 13:12

> How Lovely Shines the Morning Star
> Philip Nicolai (The *Lutheran Hymnal*, #343)

> How lovely shines the Morning Star!
> The nations see and hail afar
> The light in Judah shining.
> Thou David's Son of Jacob's race,
> My Bridegroom and my King of Grace,
> For Thee my heart is pining.
> Lowly, holy, great and glorious,
> Thou victorious Prince of graces,
> Filling all the heav'nly places.
> O highest joy by mortals won,
> True Son of God and Mary's Son,
> Thou highborn King of ages!
> Thou art my heart's most beauteous Flower,
> And Thy blest Gospel's saving power
> My raptured soul engages.

Thou mine, I Thine; sing hosanna!
Heav'nly manna tasting, eating,
Whilst Thy love in songs repeating.
Now richly to my waiting heart,
O Thou, my God, deign to impart
The grace of love undying.
In Thy blest body let me be,
E'en as the branch is in the tree,
Thy life my life supplying.
Sighing, crying, for the savor
Of Thy favor; resting never
Till I rest in Thee forever.
Lift up the voice and strike the string,
Let all glad sounds of music ring
In God's high praises blended.
Christ will be with me all the way,
Today, tomorrow, every day,
Till traveling days be ended.
Sing out, ring out, triumph glorious,
O victorious, chosen nation;
Praise the God of your salvation.
Oh, joy to know that Thou, my Friend,
Art Lord, Beginning without end,
The First and Last, eternal!
And Thou at length—O glorious grace!—
Wilt take me to that holy place,
The home of joys supernal.
Amen, Amen! Come and meet me!
Quickly greet me! With deep yearning, Lord, I look for Thy returning.

The Fifth Day

And God said, Let the waters bring forth abundantly the moving creature that hath life, and fowl *that* may fly above the earth in the open firmament of heaven. 21 And God created great whales, and every living creature that moveth, which the waters brought forth abundantly, after their kind, and every winged fowl after his kind: and God saw that *it was* good. 22 And God blessed them, saying, Be fruitful, and multiply, and fill the waters in the seas, and let fowl multiply in the earth. 23 And the evening and the morning were the fifth day. Genesis 1:20-23

God Created Whales

The greatest American novel is *Moby Dick, or The White Whale*, written by Herman Melville, who enthralled Nathaniel Hawthorne and his wife with his vivid tales, the most famous involving the story of an obsessed

Captain Ahab pursuing Moby Dick around the world. The Biblical language and allusions in the novel enrich the story, based upon allusions in the novel enrich the story, based upon historical fact of a whale attacking and sinking the Essex, whose survivors Melville met. More importantly, the novel championed the greatness, power, and intelligence of the whale.

Children find the size and power of the dinosaurs impressive, but the whale makes all other animals seem puny in comparison. Even the brontosaurus is dwarfed by the largest whales.

Moby Dick was a sperm whale, with a great square head filled with the richest source of oil. No one has concluded the exact purpose of this store of oil, whether for buoyancy or communication. Melville thought it made a marvelous battering ram. The pursuit of whale oil created an industry in England , New England , Scandinavia , and Japan .

Whale oil has been prized for the anointing of kings, for lighting lamps, for cosmetics, and recently for use in automatic transmissions. The heart of a blue whale is as large as a VW car. The aorta of the blue whale is large enough for man to stand upright in. A baby could crawl through its arteries. The strength of that heart and the volume of the blood pumped is beyond our comprehension. God designed a perfect creature for swimming the oceans, diving as deep as 2,000 feet. Several humans have reached a depth of 558 without deep diving equipment, but one died in the attempt. The whale endures incredible pressures far beyond 500, surpassed by humans only with the help of nuclear submarines, which borrow the whale's pings to navigate.

Jonah's whale became the point of contention in the doctrinal battles of the conservative Lutherans in the 1970's. Those who doubted the Book of Jonah - judging it a myth, allegory, or fable – stuck on two topics addressed by Melville himself. Skeptics have always choked on the concept of a whale swallowing a man and vomiting him on the shores of Nineveh. Both the swallowing and the express trip have troubled those who seek errors and contradictions in the Bible.

Melville was not an orthodox Christian. In fact, his novel displays the world religion notions of his Masonic relatives. However, he did address the two issues of rationalism, based on his observations and knowledge.

The swallowing seems impossible for whales and fatal for any human. Melville had another perspective: It is not necessary, hints the Bishop, that we consider Jonah as tombed in the whale's belly, but as temporarily lodged in some part of his mouth.

And this seems reasonable enough in the good Bishop. For truly, the Right Whale's mouth would accommodate a couple of whist tables, and comfortably seat all the players. Possibly, too, Jonah might have ensconced himself in a hollow tooth; but, on second thoughts, the Right Whale is toothless. (Moby *Dick*, Jonah Historically Regarded)

Melville also recorded the miraculous movement of whales across the globe. He spent years on whaling ships, observing that the ability of whales to traverse the oceans defied reason. The sailors noted the weapons they used and discussed distinctive whales they had wounded but did not kill. When the whalers compared notes or captured a previously wounded whale, the speed and length of their trips indicated a method of movement unknown to man, perhaps secret passages.

The truth of Jonah does not depend on Melville's authority that the story could happen. So much abuse has been poured upon the slender Book of Jonah that the testimony of a whale-expert skeptic to Biblical skeptics remains the ultimate irony. Neither aspect of Jonah's adventure is crucial. The range of incredible animal abilities continues to fill the latest books and television specials. No one thinks animals can do certain marvelous deeds until those marvels are filmed, explained, and viewed in slow motion. Then the miraculous becomes commonplace.

The real issue of Jonah involves God bending all of Creation to His will, by His Word. When God commanded Jonah to preach repentance to Nineveh, the prophet booked a passage for the opposite end of the earth. God sent a mighty wind to stop the ship, terrifying the suspicious sailors. They tossed goods overboard to lighten the load. They tried to row the ship to shore, because no one ventured far from shore in those days. The sailors, with fear driving their muscles, could not fight the storm. They hauled Jonah out of the hold where he was sleeping, cast lots, and identified Jonah as the reason behind the monstrous storm.

And he said unto them, I *am* an Hebrew; and I fear the LORD, the God of heaven, which hath made the sea and the dry *land.* Jonah 1:9

They did not want to throw him into the sea, but rowing failed them. Finally, they cast him into the sea.

So they took up Jonah, and cast him forth into the sea: and the sea ceased from her raging. 16 Then the men feared the LORD exceedingly, and offered a sacrifice unto the LORD, and made vows. 17 Now the LORD had prepared great fish to swallow up Jonah. And Jonah was in the belly of the fish three days and three nights. Jonah 1:15-17

The story of Jonah requires faith in the Creator, not in a whale's ability. God determined to have Nineveh repent through Jonah, so He made any other action impossible. No distant port was far enough away to be beyond the reach of God's Word. Just as God brought the prodigal prophet back through a whale, so the Triune God pursues us with His gracious Promises, using every instrument in His mighty arsenal to include us and keep us in His Kingdom.

But he answered and said unto them, An evil and adulterous generation seeketh after a sign; and there shall no sign be given to it, but the sign of the prophet Jonas: 40 For as Jonas was three days and three nights in the whale's belly; so shall the Son of man be three days and three nights in the heart of the earth. 41 The men of Nineveh shall rise in judgment with this generation, and shall condemn it: because they repented at the preaching of Jonas; and, behold, a greater than Jonas *is* here. 42 The queen of the south shall rise up in the judgment with this generation, and shall condemn it: for she came from the uttermost parts of the earth to hear the wisdom of Solomon; and, behold, a greater than Solomon *is* here. Matthew 12:39-42

Jonah foreshadowed the death and resurrection of Christ. If God cannot command a storm and a whale to remove His prophet to Nineveh, then neither can He declare believers forgiven through the merits of Christ.

Fowl That May Fly

The birds God created through the Word are constant reminders of His wisdom.

The fifth day of Creation gave us the fish of the sea and the birds of the air. Nowhere is it stated that God created lizards that evolved into birds, although the evolution-fans would have us believe it.

Birds are difficult to define. Not all of them fly. Some are great swimmers and use their wings to swim underwater. They do have one thing in common – feathers. No other creature can boast of this miracle. A television program promoting evolution simply stated that the feather is a miracle, so we must accept that verdict, although the definition is all wrong. A miracle is an event where God sets aside His own laws to benefit mankind. For instance, when the man who was blind from birth was healed by Jesus that was a miracle.

Still, it is good to think of the feather as a miracle. We see so many of them that we take them for granted. Clean a pool and feathers will be floating on it. Sweep the patio and feathers may appear in the debris. We sleep on feather pillows and rest under down comforters. Many cultures adorn themselves with feathers. Most of all we admire the great splendor of the peacock's feathers, which are hidden most of the time and glorious when displayed to prove his grandeur and territory. God has given the peacock extraordinary beauty, down to the comical topknots on his head, but deprived him of a matching voice or anything resembling intelligence.

The feather is a vital part of the bird's equipment for flight, but the Lord of Creation did not simply adorn a creature with feathers and nothing more for soaring through the clouds. Every part of the bird is uniquely designed by God for this task (although some are modified for other chores, such as diving for fish, swimming under-water, or running pell-mell across the Australian plain). The bones of a bird are hollow and light, which is why we do not allow cats and dogs to chew on them, for fear of causing terminal indigestion. Their lungs are built for the rapid breathing necessary for their great exertions. Their legs tighten up when they sleep, so they stay on branches while sound asleep. Put a flock of humans in a tree and they will fall to the ground as they slip away and lose their grip on the branches and trunk. A flashlight shining in a tree will reveal birds dosing away, secure on their branches, somewhat awakened by light but slipping back into sleep.

We use the term bird-brain to demean someone's intelligence, but birds are quite intelligent. We often associate a sense of humor with intelligence, and birds have plenty of that quality. A bird will imitate a man's limp. One photographer found the rare bird he wanted to capture for history. He got his tripod and camera ready and the bird disappeared. He looked up and found it resting on his long telescopic lens.

Birds have personalities. The blue jay is a humorous bully. He will make the sound of a hawk to scare birds from the feeder. One blue jay took his bath every day and then lit on the kitchen bird-feeder to scream at me to put the food out. He was always hilarious to see, wet and frazzled looking (no longer blue, for his feathers are not blue but refract light – when wet they are a neutral color). He always screamed in a most obnoxious, self-centered way and then flew to the tree when I opened the window to fill the tray. After that he always lit on the tray and took the best tidbits of food for himself.

The Blue jay

Blue jays share with squirrels the honor of planting oak trees. One study of blue jays showed that they were quite earnest in planting acorns without any thought of digging them up again. Thus the Creator allowed

His creatures to plant forests and to enjoy the fruits of their labor, or at least the fruit of their ancestors' labors.

A scientist was asked to summarize his work studying nature at the end of his life. He said, "God was inordinately fond of beetles." We could just as easily say He was inordinately fond of birds, because we have such a wide variety to delight us and serve us. We do not think of them often because they are constantly present. When our dogs are done with their morning breakfast, several birds hang around to pick up the scraps. At any of the outdoor venues in Phoenix, birds work the tables to pick up scraps from diners. So many of the Phoenix hardware or gardening centers are half sheltered from the sun (but easily available to birds) that birds frequently flit around the shelving. At one Home Depot, ten birds took over the charcoal grill department, cheerfully hopping from shelf to shelf.

Behold the fowls of the air: for they sow not, neither do they reap, nor gather into barns; yet your heavenly Father feedeth them. Are ye not much better than they? Matthew 6:26

Clearly Jesus, the Lord of Creation, created the birds so that they would be a centerpiece of His Sermon on the Mount. Jesus is both Creator and Preacher, reminding us with an earthly example so obviously before us at all times that we can hardly deny the truth of His wisdom.

With amazing ingenuity birds build nests of all sorts and care for their families. How does each morning start out? There is no food in storage and no promise of food for the day. Nevertheless, birds cheerfully Matins to their Creator. This wonderful chorus each morning is designed for our benefit, for God's creatures can communicate many different ways. There is a recent example of prairie dogs calling out beyond the human spectrum when they sound an alarm. Tasmanian devils make horrible sounds. Lions roar to declare their territory. Although whales chirp and make other sounds, they are beyond our hearing. What other creature sings? A singing dog is one who howls more than most. Cats screech longer and perhaps louder, but no more harmoniously.

Except for the peacock, the one animal we associate with beautiful singing is the bird. Birds do not sing the same song but join in a wonderful chorus in the morning, allowing us to pick out the various songs. A blue jay may screech to get some food, but he will make a unique bell-like sound when he is happy. Cardinals and robins have beautiful calls. The hummingbird is not a singer but he more than makes up for it by flitting about and showing off his jeweled vest. Gardeners brag about hummingbirds that fly close to them, even seeming to peer in their faces. The flying rainbows seem to know who feeds them and cares for their favorite flowers.

These birds start each day with nothing to eat and yet they sing God's praises. They use their intelligence to build homes useful for their children but they rely on nothing but God's generosity to feed them. They lack the ability to store fat and water in their bodies.

Jesus' comparison is aimed at making us see how cheerful the birds are. And He asks us, "Are you not much better than these birds? The Heavenly Father cares for them, and He will care for you as well."

In the novel *Vanity Fair* (its name borrowed from *Pilgrim's Progress*) William Makepeace Thackeray wrote about the energies expended by people who were so anxious to get an estate. One chapter is titled "How To Live Well on Nothing a Year." It told how the young couple kept creditors at bay by hinting that a great estate was coming to them.

In so many fake religious works of today we are urged to have more faith that prosperity will follow. But what faith is being promoted? Faith in ourselves and not in God. They advocate the cleverness of man, not the wisdom of God. It is no surprise that these fake religious leaders are so full of themselves. They have followed their own advice and find themselves living in great luxury with many people bowing to them. The novel *Vanity Fair* reminds us of those same symptoms. In old England, everyone was measured by his annual income and his team of horses. Now it is annual income and horsepower (the car's). Several people were shocked at the extraordinary income of a synod vice-president ($100,000 per year). The synod presidents receive $200,000 per year and who-knows-how-many perks, such as free trips around the US and the world. The splendor is not considered a mark against them but proof of their infernal cleverness in gaining the advantage over their political opponents. So they sneer at pastors and congregations who want to be faithful, even if it means being poor in comparison.

Anxiety is a mental condition caused in part by one's limited faith in God. It is true that the weakest faith still holds the complete treasure of the Gospel. However, a weak faith will easily let go of the treasure if the Gospel seems to be getting in the way of inner peace. Thus we need constant reminders not to be anxious. The birds of the air are never anxious. They go about their duties with great cheerfulness. The coyote lurks and sneaks around, hoping for a meal and worried about being shot. A bird will do his work with great trust and courage. A flock of birds will appoint several to man the picket. One will light on the ground, then another. If they are undisturbed, the rest follow. Likewise the rapid and noisy exit of one bird will alarm the flock and send them all into the air, whether they see the danger or not. Then the sentinels return, one at a time, until the whole flocks feels good about landing again.

Birds know their benefactors. Many who drive to feed birds will learn that the birds in question (ducks, blue birds) will make their happy Shriners'

Convention noises when they hear that one particular engine (and no other). A flock of birds will chortle among themselves while waiting for a gardener to finish working a worm and bug rich area of fresh soil.. Similarly, if a large amount of food is scattered on the ground regularly, the dominant birds of the area will settle in and wait for their main meal. Someone called them *Entitlement Birds;* waiting for the meals they felt owed to them.

Every land has its rare beauties in the bird population to admire, its commoners to despise. Most of us would love to have the parrots they enjoy in Australia. We look down on the common grackles and starlings that thrive everywhere. In Midland I saw the grackles slowly work the lawn, pulling out grubs with their powerful beaks. They are corvids, relatives of the cagey crows, lacking in colorful beauty but overflowing in intelligence. One grackle will watch out for another, calling to the one in danger. Starlings are also related and equally despised. Worst of all, they travel in great flocks. What harm do they do? They walk through a garden (in a comical drunken gait) and fish around for insects under the mulch. Ask a boy or a man to look for every insect in the mulch and that helper will cry out in pain. The birds search for pests with great alacrity and skill.

God's wisdom can be shown in how He plans the eruption of the bug population during that time when birds must feed their young. Insects are the mutton, poultry, and beef of the bird's table. Robins will tug at the lowly earthworm and feed it to the children, but the favorite meal for most birds (doves excepted) is insect meat. (Doves digest seed and give their children "dove milk" or half-digested seed. These seeds are weeds for the most part.) Why give bird's food and water? So they stay in the yard and patrol for insects. They do not become dependent on man's food, which is only 15% of their diet at most. But they do survive the winter better and feed their young more effectively with some help.

A jay can be quite raucous in demanding food. In New Ulm, there was a different bird to tend. I scattered sunflower seeds on the front feeder whenever I could. One day I went out to do an errand. A pretty robin stepped out on the branch and chirped at me, not in a demanding but in a reminding sort of call. I went inside and got her ration of seed. It was nesting time, so a snack of sunflowers had to be good for the parents.

We should stop in wonder when we think of the complexity of God's Creation. For instance, people will generalize about a problem and produce one rather rigid solution. For instance, the solution for teen alcoholism is to stop the companies from advertising, as if there is one cause and one effect. How can we generalize about birds? They live in many different zones. Some burrow in the ground (or occupy burrows). Some live in the highest trees, others midway, still others in bushes near the ground. Many birds are content to nest on the ground. Birds do not like to compete with their own kind in a given area, but they tolerate other species. The result is that we can have birds nesting at each level of our yard and feeding at various levels, allowing a fairly large population to be sheltered with the proper plants, water, and food.

The birds of the air do not sow, reap, or gather into barns, but the Heavenly Father takes care of them. The message of this verse is that God will take care of us, too. It is a small matter for Him. He sent His beloved Son into our world to redeem us from sin, to die on the cross and rise from the dead. In comparison, our material needs are nothing for God to supply.

Knowing that Jesus is the Lord of Creation helps us to be thankful for the blessings around us day by day. If we feel sad, oppressed, and worried, a remedy is provided for us in the joyous singing of the birds. How can we not think about God creating these wonderful animals? How can we not think of His care for each and everyone of us. It is not enough that He cares for us. He wants our lives to be full, complete, satisfying, filled with joy, humor, and love.

All Things Bright and Beautiful

Refrain

All things bright and beautiful,
All creatures great and small,
All things wise and wonderful:
The Lord God made them all.

Each little flower that opens,
Each little bird that sings,
He made their glowing colors,
He made their tiny wings.

Refrain

The rich man in his castle,
The poor man at his gate,
He made them, high or lowly,
And ordered their estate.

Refrain

The purple headed mountains,
The river running by,
The sunset and the morning
That brightens up the sky.

Refrain

The cold wind in the winter,
The pleasant summer sun,
The ripe fruits in the garden,
He made them every one.

Refrain

The tall trees in the greenwood,
The meadows where we play,
The rushes by the water,
To gather every day.

Refrain

He gave us eyes to see them,
And lips that we might tell
How great is God Almighty,
Who has made all things well.

Refrain

Birds We Love

Robin

The most loved bird of America may be the robin as the herald of Spring. In cold climates the snow, ice, sleet, and cold make winter a long ordeal. The sighting of the first robin of spring is a common game for people to enjoy. The robins appear in small numbers at first, while the snow is still melting away. They wear their sweaters in the cold weather. The birds look strangely bulky, using their feathers fluffed out to keep their bodies warm.

Although people think of feathers as an essential ingredient for flying, the use of feathers for warmth has attracted man's attention since the earliest times. Down comforters, jackets, and slippers are ideal for warmth, softness, and lightness: unmatched in luxury by any man-made fiber. Feathers are not only a marvel for their complex design in making flight possible, but also in trapping air to maintain bodily warmth. The downy feather is especially soft to the touch, a tiny emblem of divine purpose.

The robin's cheerful song is just as much a trademark as its habit of pulling up earthworms for its nesting children. The lawns of America have provided a boon for the robin population, harboring an endless supply of worms for a hungry population of chirping nestlings. If a robin builds a nest within easy reach, the script for feeding can be observed easily. When the tiny birds see an object over their heads – even a human hand - they reach up together with their beaks open, chirping for food while looking like a choir of earnest singers, raising their voices to Heaven.

Because the robin brings in the spring, feeds its young close to humans, and offers such a cheerful song, the robin best represents the home and family, devotion to children, and the tireless energy of caring parents.

The Savior created birds to serve many different purposes, including our entertainment and edification. No other creature is so numerous and delightful at the same time. When foreign potentates visited the throne of the Byzantine Empire , they were astounded to see a golden tree with jeweled mechanical birds singing in different voices. The mechanical marvel of that opulent court was nothing compared to the constant glory of birds throughout the world. People stop and ask when they visit a new region, "Which bird is that?"

The humming bird is one favorite we all know on sight, although there are many different varieties. They are the most entertaining of all birds because they have no fear. People have reported seeing hummers racing their cars down the road, but a more common sight is the personal greeting. A humming bird will not only fly back and forth through the spray of a garden hose, but also fly up to the face of gardener and hover in an amused and unhurried way. Seeing a humming bird so close is so rewarding and gratifying that it becomes a bragging point for bird lovers, especially since hummers seem to favor those who do the most for them.

The Hummingbird

People love to attract hummers, so they buy feeders and fill them with sugar water, whose spigots are promptly attacked by bees and ants. Although the birds will show great appreciation for the feeders and even return to that space to look for them, they love natural food even more. Hummers cannot exist on sugar water anymore than humans can. They need insects for long-term energy. The best plan for a humming bird haven concentrates on natural feeding stations – the flowers they love most. They will dip into any flower for nectar and insects, but they seem to prefer small red blooms the most. They feast at:

- Impatiens
- Bergamot (Oswego Tea)
- French horticultural bean flowers
- Cannas
- Cape honeysuckle
- Hibiscus

Hummers and all birds need shelter. Bushes provide a great hiding place for the tiny humming bird nest, which is as tiny as a half walnut shell. Pussy willows are a favorite ingredient for their nests. All birds appreciate string, yarn, animal fur, and mud for their nests. The Savior designed all His creatures - except modern man – to recycle with 100% efficiency.

An ideal yard will feature a fountain for birds. Birds want a safe place to bathe: shallow, noisy, splashing water. Hummers prefer a mist to fly through. They can get their shower safely on the fly and then preen in the seclusion of a nearby tree or bush.

All Praise to Thee

Thomas Ken

All praise to Thee, my God, this night,
For all the blessings of the light!
Keep me, O keep me, King of kings,
Beneath Thine own almighty wings.

Forgive me, Lord, for Thy dear Son,
The ill that I this day have done,
That with the world, myself, and Thee,
I, ere I sleep, at peace may be.

O when shall I, in endless day,
For ever chase dark sleep away,
And hymns divine with angels sing,
All praise to thee, eternal King?

Praise God, from Whom all blessings flow;
Praise Him, all creatures here below;
Praise Him above, ye heavenly host;
Praise Father, Son, and Holy Ghost.
(The *Lutheran Hymnal*, #558)

The Sixth Day

And God said, Let the earth bring forth the living creature after his kind, cattle, and creeping thing, and beast of the earth after his kind: and it was so. 25 And God made the beast of the earth after his kind, and cattle after their kind, and every thing that creepeth upon the earth after his kind: and God saw that *it was* good. 26 And God said, Let us make man in our image, after our likeness: and let them have dominion over the fish of the sea, and over the fowl of the air, and over the cattle, and over all the earth, and over every creeping thing that creepeth upon the earth. 27 So God created man in his *own* image, in the image of God created he him; male and female created he them. 28 And God blessed them, and God said unto them, Be fruitful, and multiply, and replenish the earth, and subdue it: and have dominion over the fish of the sea, and over the fowl of the air, and over every living thing that moveth upon the earth. 29 And God said, Behold, I have given you every herb bearing seed, which *is* upon the face of all the earth, and every tree, in the which *is* the fruit of a tree yielding seed; to you it shall be for meat. 30 And to every beast of the earth, and to every fowl of the air, and to every thing that creepeth upon the earth, wherein *there is* life, *I have given* every green herb for meat: and it was so. 31 And God saw every thing that he had made, and, behold, *it was* very good. And the evening and the morning were the sixth day . Genesis 1:24-31

"Let us make man in our image."

No chapter in the Old Testament speaks so clearly of the Holy Trinity as Genesis 1. The Word of God reveals this in the plainest language, with a combination of the plural and the singular. God speaks through the Word, which we know from John 1 to be the Son of God. The Holy Spirit broods over the waters. And yet it is God, one God, who speaks – the unity of the Three Persons, the Three-ness of the One God. The word for God itself is a plural form, and God said, "Let us make man in our image."

The evolutionary view of worship holds that primitive man worshiped many gods until monotheism was invented, with only one God. The evolutionists normally progress to atheism, which they find even more refined and intellectual than monotheism. However, just as a mighty empire like Rome can crumble into a dozen primitive feudal societies, so also can the pure religion of God decay into polytheism, animism, cults, and fads of the moment. Christ did not teach the creation of 400 denominations but one faith only, yet man has subdivided that singular brilliant truth into hundreds of shadowy teachings emphasizing one error or another. How many people have grown up under the supposed teachings of Christianity and yet have heard only the Law, never imagining that Jesus taught forgiveness and love rather than condemnation and guilt?

We often say that God made man in His image, but the Scriptures say, "in our image." We should constantly reflect on this, because the revelation of the Holy Trinity in the Bible is unique among all the religions of the world. Therefore, it is correct to say "in His image" even though the words of Genesis say "in our image." The Holy Trinity is a mystery revealed to us. Once believers know this mystery, the Scriptures become a mine filled with treasure. No matter which way we turn, the veins of precious metal run deeper and deeper. We can never exhaust the vast supply. In fact, the more we delve, the more opens up to us. Attacks against this truth only strengthen the faith of believers, who have known and experienced the nature of God. All the subordinate works of faith help support the essentials revealed in the Bible, for there is a vast cloud of witnesses to these truths.

When all the great and wise men of the world clamor against God or become silent and apathetic, when all the trials of Job fall upon the believer, the attributes of God remain the same as they have been since Creation. The objective truths of the Scriptures can never be refuted, for they are revealed through the Holy Spirit and hidden from the blind attackers.

Every believer knows he is made in the image of God. Pagans comfort or terrify themselves with the images of dragons, rats, and monsters, but the Bible speaks to us of:

His eyes:

But Noah found grace in the eyes of the LORD. Genesis 6:8

He ruleth by his power for ever; his eyes behold the nations: let not the rebellious exalt themselves. Selah. Psalm 66:7

O LORD, *are* not thine eyes upon the truth? Jeremiah 5:3

His arm:

Wherefore say unto the children of Israel, I *am* the LORD, and I will bring you out from under the burdens of the Egyptians, and I will rid you out of their bondage, and I will redeem you with a stretched out arm, and with great judgments: Exodus 6:6

The LORD hath made bare his holy arm in the eyes of all the nations; and all the ends of the earth shall see the salvation of our God. Isaiah 52:10

Who hath believed our report? and to whom is the arm of the LORD revealed? Isaiah 53:1

That the saying of Esaias the prophet might be fulfilled, which he spake, Lord, who hath believed our report? and to whom hath the arm of the Lord been revealed? John 12:38

His hand:

Behold, the hand of the LORD is upon thy cattle which *is* in the field, upon the horses, upon the asses, upon the camels, upon the oxen, and uponthe sheep: *there shall be* a very grievous murrain. Exodus 9:3

And the hand of the LORD was on Elijah; and he girded up his loins, and ran before Ahab to the entrance of Jezreel. 1 Kings 18:46

Thou shalt also be a crown of glory in the hand of the LORD, and a royal diadem in the hand of thy God. Isaiah 62:3

And all they that heard *them* laid *them* up in their hearts, saying, What manner of child shall this be! And the hand of the Lord was with him. Luke 1:66

And the hand of the Lord was with them: and a great number believed, and turned unto the Lord. Acts 11:21

His ears:

LORD, bow down thine ear, and hear: open, LORD, thine eyes, and see: and hear the words of Sennacherib, which hath sent him to reproach the living God. 2 Kings 19:16

Give ear, O LORD, unto my prayer; and attend to the voice of my supplications. Psalm 86:6

His mouth:

And the glory of the LORD shall be revealed, and all flesh shall see *it* together: for the mouth of the LORD hath spoken *it* . Isaiah 40:5

Thus saith the LORD of hosts, Hearken not unto the words of the prophets that prophesy unto you: they make you vain: they speak a vision of their own heart, *and* not out of the mouth of the LORD. Jeremiah 23:16

His voice:

And they heard the voice of the LORD God walking in the garden in the cool of the day: and Adam and his wife hid themselves from the presence of the LORD God amongst the trees of the garden. **Genesis 3:8**

And said, If thou wilt diligently hearken to the voice of the LORD thy God, and wilt do that which is right in his sight, and wilt give ear to his commandments, and keep all his statutes, I will put none of these diseases upon thee, which I have brought upon the Egyptians: for I *am* the LORD that healeth thee. **Exodus 15:26**

The voice of the LORD *is* powerful; the voice of the LORD *is* full of majesty. **Psalm 29:4**

Whether *it be* good, or whether *it be* evil, we will obey the voice of the LORD our God, to whom we send thee; that it may be well with us, when we obey the voice of the LORD our God. **Jeremiah 42:6**

His thoughts, mind:

The counsel of the LORD standeth for ever, the thoughts of his heart to all generations. **Psalm 33:11**

How precious also are thy thoughts unto me, O God! how great is the sum of them! **Psalm 139:17**

For my thoughts *are* not your thoughts, neither *are* your ways my ways, saith the LORD. 9 For *as* the heavens are higher than the earth, so are my ways higher than your ways, and my thoughts than your thoughts. **Isaiah 55:8-9**

O the depth of the riches both of the wisdom and knowledge of God! how unsearchable *are* his judgments, and his ways past finding out! 34 For who hath known the mind of the Lord? or who hath been his counsellor? 35 Or who hath first given to him, and it shall be recompensed unto him again? 36 For of him, and through him, and to him, *are* all things: to whom *be* glory for ever. Amen. **Romans 11:33-36**

The Romans 11 passage is one of the key Trinitarian passages of the New Testament, with two allusions to the Trinity. Verse 33 exalts literally about the depth: of the riches, wisdom, and knowledge of God. If we would write in the verbose manner of man rather than the concise language of the Holy Spirit, the verse would read:

The depth of riches,

The depth of the wisdom, and the depth of the knowledge of God.

The language of the Holy Spirit is not at all improved by prolixity, but the Trinitarian form of the verse is made clearer. Verse 36 is more apparently Trinitarian, with three references to Him. Have people wondered why Western man prefers so many lists of three? Why do we give three reasons for everything? Why do we group all manner of objects in three? The three-ness of God permeates our understanding, even when we do not acknowledge its original source.

The spiritually blind see God created in man's image, but man was created in God's image. The human attributes of God in the Scriptures are easily overlooked by believers, who hear these terms so frequently in the appointed lessons and sermons. They reveal God as close to us, not remote, as compassionate in His understanding and mercy, not as cold and cruel. The pagan false gods demanded human sacrifice, even the destruction of their own children. Ancient historians record how one city felt their military losses were due to their neglect of child sacrifice, substituting servants' children for their own. To appease their angry god they killed their own children in great numbers.

God's identification with man became complete when God became flesh, born of the Virgin Mary. When people heard Jesus speaking in His public ministry, they experienced what Moses found at the Burning Bush: two natures in one. Moses saw a bush on fire, but the bush was not consumed. The duality of the burning bush foreshadowed the Two Natures—divine and human—of the Incarnation, for the Son of God spoke from the bush.

And God said unto Moses, I AM THAT I AM: and he said, Thus shalt thou say unto the children of Israel, I AM hath sent me unto you. 15 And God said moreover unto Moses, Thus shalt thou say unto the children of Israel, The LORD God of your fathers, the God of Abraham, the God of Isaac, and the God of Jacob, hath sent me unto you: this *is* my name for ever, and this *is* my memorial unto all generations. Exodus 3:14-15

The Angel of the Lord (Exodus 3:2) was more than an angel, because He identified Himself as God in Exodus 3:14-15.

When Abraham was faithful to the command to sacrifice his beloved son, the Angel of the Lord stopped him and supplied a substitute:

And the angel of the LORD called unto him out of heaven, and said, Abraham, Abraham: and he said, Here *am* I. 12 And he said,

Lay not thine hand upon the lad, neither do thou any thing unto him: for now I know that thou fearest God, seeing thou hast not withheld thy son, thine only *son* from me. Genesis 22:11-12

Moreover, when Jacob wrestled with a man at the Jabbok, he said he wrestled with God.

And Jacob called the name of the place Peniel [face of God]: for I have seen God face to face, and my life is preserved. Genesis 32:30

Then said the Jews unto him, Thou art not yet fifty years old, and hast thou seen Abraham? 58 Jesus said unto them, Verily, verily, I say unto you, Before Abraham was, I am. 59 Then took they up stones to cast at him: but Jesus hid himself, and went out of the temple, going through the midst of them, and so passed by. John 8:57-59

Jesus clearly identified Himself with the voice of the Burning Bush, the Angel of the Lord. He gave His own people the opportunity to hear the voice of God expressed at their level. Although man fell into sin through Adam and Eve, man was redeemed by the God-man Jesus Christ. The strength of Christianity is its ability to reach all ages, all stations in life, with the revelation of God being born in meekness and poverty, giving up the glory of Heaven to give the riches of His grace to man.

Man in His Own Image

Genesis 1:27 So God created man in his *own* image, in the image of God created he him; male and female created he them. 28 And God blessed them, and God said unto them, Be fruitful, and multiply, and replenish the earth, and subdue it: and have dominion over the fish of the sea, and over the fowl of the air, and over every living thing that moveth upon the earth.

God created man perfect, something we can hardly imagine today. We see the Old Adam in children from the beginning. The first word spoken with the most frequency by the majority of children is "No!" They have already heard it so often that they know exactly how to say the word with emphasis. Young parents are often shocked at the will power of the tiny creature.

When God created Adam and Eve, he gave them the freedom to decide between right and wrong. People admire animals because those creatures do not decide these matters and therefore look innocent in comparison with man. However, man would have to be robotic to live up – or rather down – to the same conditions. What scientists call instinct is another name for God hard-coding commands into animals. The mother cat carries her kittens to safety because she was designed to do that. Later on the same cat will see her grown children as rivals and fight them. The noblest impulses of animals are insights into what man is capable of doing, a far more difficult task because of that freedom and the Old Adam.

Augustine spoke eloquently to our generation of self-esteem advocates:

Why is so much assumed about the ability of human nature? It has been wounded, hurt, injured, ruined. It has need of a true confession, not of a false defense. (Augustine, *De natura et gratia* , chap. 53; quoted with approval by Chemnitz, *Examination of the Council of Trent* , 1971, I, p. 411).

The more freedom we have, the less we appreciate it. The richest people should be the most accomplished and sympathetic in the world. The opposite is true. Trust fund babies have all the chances one could have to be generous and to achieve without the burden of making of living. They are thrust into Paradise, without planning or earning it, and they take advantage by using their freedom as a license.

Adam and Eve were given one specific command not to do something – eat from the forbidden fruit – so they went to it and ate, tempted by Satan to become like God, knowing good and evil.

With this sin came a three-fold curse.

1. Satan was cursed for tempting Adam and Eve. The serpent would no longer be beautiful and attractive but repulsive and frightening. Even today it is the symbol of evil.

2. Adam was cursed with a lifetime of hard labor. Instead of casually collecting his food he would have to sweat for it and fight the brambles, weeds, and thorns.

3. Eve was cursed with difficulty in childbirth for being beguiled by Satan.

Yet God also promised Adam and Eve the Savior. In those three curses would a three-fold blessing be woven. Satan would play his part by bruising the Savior and having his nefarious head crushed. The Savior would crush Satan and trample death under His feet.

And the LORD God said unto the serpent, Because thou hast done this, thou *art* cursed above all cattle, and above every beast of the field; upon thy belly shalt thou go, and dust shalt thou eat all the days of thy life: 15 And I will put enmity between thee and the woman, and between thy seed and her seed; it shall bruise thy head, and thou shalt bruise his heel. 16 Unto the woman he said, I will greatly multiply thy sorrow and thy conception; in sorrow thou shalt bring forth children; and thy desire *shall be* to thy husband, and he shall rule over thee. Genesis 3:14-16

The Old Adam would be defeated by the New Adam: since by man came death, by man came also the resurrection.

KJV 1 Corinthians 15:21 For since by man *came* death, by man *came* also the resurrection of the dead. 22 For as in Adam all die, even so in Christ shall all be made alive. 23 But every man in his own order: Christ the firstfruits; afterward they that are Christ's at his coming. 24 Then *cometh* the end, when he shall have delivered up the kingdom to God, even the Father; when he shall have put down all rule and all authority and power. 25 For he must reign, till he hath put all enemies under his feet.

Eve became a symbol of the Virgin Mary, who was like Eve before the Fall, yet in need of a Savior because of her sin. The Savior was born of a woman, conceived by the Holy Spirit and born in the flesh. In this and many other aspects, Christianity is unique. God acts in history, intervenes in our troubled affairs, and send His only Son to be our Savior and Redeemer.

The Lost Sheep

The Seventh Day

Thus the heavens and the earth were finished, and all the host of them. 2 And on the seventh day God ended his work which he had made; and he rested on the seventh day from all his work which he had made. 3 And God blessed the seventh day, and sanctified it: because that in it he had rested from all his work which God created and made. Genesis 2:1-3

God created the Sabbath laws to set the family free and to keep the family close to Him. For most of world history, man has labored to stay alive and feed his family. Until the mechanical age, most labor has been agricultural with great demands made upon every member of the household. The commandment to rest on the Sabbath and keep it holy was a boon to the husband, to let him get by with the least of his required chores. The commandment set his wife free from preparing meals and cleaning the home. The children and servants did not have to step in for the husband and wife, and the animals themselves were rested. One Mennonite farmer explained his viewpoint simply, "If I cannot get a week's work done in six days, then I won't get it done in seven." He never worked on Sunday and prospered more than his neighbors who did.

Six days shalt thou labour, and do all thy work: 10 But the seventh day *is* the sabbath of the LORD thy God: *in it* thou shalt not do any work, thou, nor thy son, nor thy daughter, thy manservant, nor thy maidservant, nor thy cattle, nor thy stranger that *is* within thy gates: 11 For *in* six days the LORD made heaven and earth, the sea, and all that in them *is* , and rested the seventh day: wherefore the LORD blessed the sabbath day, and hallowed it. Exodus 20:9-11

The purpose of the Sabbath is rest, togetherness, study, and worship. Today all three are lacking in the lives of many. When people are ill, the doctors prescribe rest. When the troubles of life seem to overwhelm, rest is often the best medicine as well. Physicians now induce artificial comas simply for the sake of healing, and ancient doctors used the same practice to cure difficult problems. Likewise, time together is often so lacking in a family that judges have been known to command certain activities for parents and children. Sunday, the last bastion of togetherness has been leveled simply because so few care to honor and keep sacred the day of worship. Nothing is valued as well as it might be, until it is taken away. A super abundance is even more likely to lead us into antipathy, not because of the abundance but because of our fallen nature. Worship should be our greatest treasure in life because no one can take it away from us, even if money, property, and lives are confiscated. Worship transcends all earthly value because God speaks directly to us. In the Law He thunders at us and shows us our abundant faults. In the Gospel Promises, the Triune God converts us into believers and then strengthens our weak faith throughout life.

Every worship service has a special choir, which joins us in our praise of God.

But ye are come unto mount Zion, and unto the city of the living God, the heavenly Jerusalem, and to an innumerable company of angels, 23 To the general assembly and church of the firstborn, which are written in heaven, and to God the Judge of all, and to the spirits of just men made perfect, 24 And to Jesus the mediator of the new covenant, and to the blood of sprinkling, that speaketh better things than *that of* Abel. Hebrews 12:22-24

When the congregation is worshiping, the heavens open up and angels mingle their divine chorus with our earthly singing. As the members look about, they see everything fashioned by Jesus the Creating Word – leather on their Bibles, paper in the hymnals, wool, cotton, and linen, stone, and metals. Christ is the foremost guest in the service, promising to be with the tiniest group, even two or three.

For where two or three are gathered together in my name, there am I in the midst of them. Matthew 18:20

The liturgical service is where Creation and Redemption come together. The original Six Day Creation was perfect, but man used his free will to sin against God. Nevertheless, God promised the Messiah to Adam and Eve as they were being expelled from the Garden of Eden. They lost the earthly Paradise, but the Messiah would give mankind the heavenly Paradise. Everyone in the Old Testament who believed in the coming Messiah was justified by faith; there is just as much Gospel in the Old

Testament as in the New Testament, perhaps more. The hundreds of Messianic passages in Old Testament are all Gospel. The passages of hope and comfort are Gospel. The shepherd passages all point to their fulfillment in the Good Shepherd.

The Psalm we memorized as children is a Gospel proclamation about the coming Messiah.

The LORD *is* my shepherd;

I shall not want.

2 He maketh me to lie down in green pastures:

he leadeth me beside the still waters.

3 He restoreth my soul:

he leadeth me in the paths of righteousness for his name's sake.

4 Yea, though I walk through the valley of the shadow of death, I will fear no evil: for thou *art* with me;
thy rod and thy staff they comfort me.

5 Thou preparest a table before me in the presence of mine enemies:

> thou anointest my head with oil;
>
> my cup runneth over.
>
> 6 Surely goodness and mercy shall follow me all the days of my life:
>
> and I will dwell in the house of the LORD for ever. Psalm 23:1

The gentleness of the Savior is described in Isaiah:

> **He shall feed his flock like a shepherd:**
> **he shall gather the lambs with his arm,**
> **and carry them in his bosom,**
> ***and* shall gently lead those that are with young.**
> **Isaiah 40:12**

Psalm 22 describes exactly how Christ would redeem the fallen world, so we can see how God prepared Israel over the centuries to understand, discern, and believe in the Messiah when He came.

My God, my God, why hast thou forsaken me? *why art thou so* far from helping me, *and from* the words of my roaring?

7 All they that see me laugh me to scorn: they shoot out the lip, they shake the head, *saying,* 8 He trusted on the LORD *that* he would deliver him: let him deliver him, seeing he delighted in him.

14 I am poured out like water, and all my bones are out of joint: my heart is like wax; it is melted in the midst of my bowels. 15 My strength is dried up like a potsherd; and my tongue cleaveth to my jaws; and thou hast brought me into the dust of death.

18 They part my garments among them, and cast lots upon my vesture.

Isaiah 53 also portrays the Good Shepherd's crucifixion, so vividly that every child recognizes the subject of the passage, written centuries before fulfillment, read aloud in the Temple and synagogues, centuries before these events happened.

He is despised and rejected of men; a man of sorrows, and acquainted with grief: and we hid as it were *our* faces from him; he was despised, and we esteemed him not. 4 Surely he hath borne our

griefs, and carried our sorrows: yet we did esteem him stricken, smitten of God, and afflicted. 5 But he *was* wounded for our transgressions, *he was* bruised for our iniquities: the chastisement of our peace *was* upon him; and with his stripes we are healed. 6 All we like sheep have gone astray; we have turned every one to his own way; and the LORD hath laid on him the iniquity of us all. 7 He was oppressed, and he was afflicted, yet he opened not his mouth: he is brought as a lamb to the slaughter, and as a sheep before her shearers is dumb, so he openeth not his mouth. 8 He was taken from prison and from judgment: and who shall declare his generation? for he was cut off out of the land of the living: for the transgression of my people was he stricken. 9 And he made his grave with the wicked, and with the rich in his death; because he had done no violence, neither *was any* deceit in his mouth. Isaiah 53:3-9

Figs from Thistles

Beware of false prophets, which come to you in sheep's clothing, but inwardly they are ravening wolves. 16 Ye shall know them by their fruits. Do men gather grapes of thorns, or figs of thistles? 17 Even so every good tree bringeth forth good fruit; but a corrupt tree bringeth forth evil fruit. 18 A good tree cannot bring forth evil fruit, neither *can* a corrupt tree bring forth good fruit. 19 Every tree that

bringeth not forth good fruit is hewn down, and cast into the fire. 20 Wherefore by their fruits ye shall know them. 21 Not every one that saith unto me, Lord, Lord, shall enter into the kingdom of heaven; but he that doeth the will of my Father which is in heaven. 22 Many will say to me in that day, Lord, Lord, have we not prophesied in thy name? and in thy name have cast out devils? and in thy name done many wonderful works? 23 And then will I profess unto them, I never knew you: depart from me, ye that work iniquity. Matthew 7:15-23

In this Gospel we have a very clear distinction between sound doctrine and false doctrine. We need to pay attention to the warning about false doctrine, but we also need to take comfort in knowing that God's Word will bear fruit, as Jesus promises us in this lesson. Although the lesson is primarily a warning, it is also a promise of God bringing about His will through His Word.

I ordered seed and distributed it in the congregation, so I am especially aware of the difference between the good seed we all want and the weed seeds we try to destroy. One tends to displace the other, as I learned from various experts. For instance, if beans are planted in a narrow file, most of the garden is open soil, where the sun strikes the weed seeds buried or blown in. If the beans have enough moisture to germinate and grow, the weeds have enough to grow as well. Therefore, the narrow bean rows are often smothered in the rank growth of well-watered weeds growing in newly tilled soil. However, if wide rows of beans are planted, they quickly cover up the open areas and smother many (but not all) of the weeds, simply by shading the soil.

Because Lutherans have neglected their own doctrine and confessions, they have left open wide areas for false teachers to spread their weed seed. In contrast, when the Scriptures and Confession are predominant in a congregation, false doctrine will erupt but it will be smothered by the overwhelming force of people clinging to the orthodox faith and comparing it to what is being secretly promoted. No one ever says: "I am going to attack the divinity of Christ, or I will overturn justification by faith. The most dangerous books against the Bible are written by clergy and bear pious names, such as: *The Bible, Book of Faith*, introduced in the ALC to destroy trust in the inerrancy of the Word.

The Lord Jesus Christ gives us several vivid comparisons, many of which remain in our current speech. How often do we hear the phrase "a wolf in sheep's clothing"? It is quite fitting, because false teachers always seem to be like sheep, soft and warm, meek and mild. This is their cloak but it does not change their substance. If a wolf in sheep's clothing is asked about sound doctrine, his eyes flash with anger and he will engage in a hostile personal attack. Or he may be terribly offended that anyone dared to ask him such a question. (That alone should make the sheep run away before they are devoured, but they often stay for dinner.) In one case, far removed from the Lutheran Church, the president of the Southern Baptist denomination, about 10 million strong, asked the Southern Baptist Louisville seminary what they taught about the Virgin Birth of Christ and other doctrinal matters. The faculty told the president, in an obvious rebuke, "It is none of your business what we teach."

How many times people have defended a false teacher by saying, "He is not a false teacher. He is a nice guy"! A few have said, "He is my classmate." One said, "I drank a lot of beer with him." All of these defenses are irrelevant. Many church members fall prey to this illusion because they say, "Oh, but I like him so much." In contrast, it is also significant to remember that the Word of God is not to be judged by what we feel when we hear it. If the unrepentant hear the Law of God, they become angry. Does that nullify the Law? They will often say, "He offended me." Some will say, "The pastor is correct, but I don't like the way he expresses himself." The wolf knows this and makes sure that his promotion of false doctrine strikes a cord in the heart-strings of his victims.

Now I beseech you, brethren, mark them which cause divisions and offences contrary to the doctrine which ye have learned; and avoid them. 18 For they that are such serve not our Lord Jesus Christ, but their own belly; and by good words and fair speeches deceive the hearts of the simple. Romans 16:17-18

False teachers are belly worshipers (lovers of comfort) and use seductive speech and flattering words to deceive the simple. For instance, the faculty of Fuller Seminary told the Wisconsin Synod and LCMS leaders that the Church Growth Movement was ideal for conservative Protestant churches like theirs. The CGM was "doctrinally neutral" and would not change the synods except to make them grow like kudzu vine. In effect they said, "Give us all your mission outreach money and we will train your leaders and pastors to be effective. Your congregations will grow and your denomination will soar in size and money. You will get the glory." However, WELS membership graph in the last 10 years looks like the big waterslide north of us. The slope is rapidly downhill and does not account for the easy-come easy-go members recently taken in with a few quick lessons. Almost all the denominations are exactly the same, and they say, "But look at all the money we have."

The second vivid comparison comes when Jesus asks about the fruits of teachers. "You will know them by their fruits. Do you gather figs from thistles or grapes from thorns?"

This comparison is very compelling for gardeners. I have a yard with two kinds of plants: weeds and flowers. Both produce seed. But I do not know of anyone who values weed seed. In fact, many gardeners go out of their way to rid themselves of weeds bearing seed. Although the weed plants and weed seed together can be seen as organic mulch or fodder for the compost, many people shudder at the thought of multiplying such dreadnaughts as goat's head, ragweed, London rocket, thistle, witch grass, or dandelion.

Weeds are famous for one thing: rank growth. Water a yard and the plants will thrive, but the weeds will erupt, spreading across the grass, like creeping Charlie (Jill over ground, a mint) or shooting up to smother tall plants, the way pigweed or ragweed will grow. No one has ever said to me, "How did you get your weeds to grow so well? May I have some seed?" Weeds produce but their yield is worthless even if abundant.

This may seem obvious, but the obvious needs to be transferred to the religious life. A thistle will never produce a fig. A thorn will never grow a grape. All the apologies for false teachers are shattered by this basic reality of how God's Word yields good fruit but Satan's word produces worthless and useless seed. Therefore, a sound teacher will always produce the fruit of the Gospel and a false teacher will always produce nothing of value.

We can see this many times over in the history of the Church. Whenever men faithfully proclaim the Word of God, the fruits of the Gospel always come forth. People believe in Christ, receive the forgiveness of sin, and inherit eternal life. Salvation is not without benefit to others, because the fruits of the Spirit produce many blessings, including love, joy, peace, and generosity toward those in need. Most people forget that the basic institutions of charity in America today were begun as Lutheran charities, because conservative Lutherans did not want the Gospel to be lost. They called this the Inner Mission and were very suspicious of those who wanted to do works without teaching the Word of God. (This was originally called Social Service by the Lutherans but we remember it by the later name used – the Social Gospel Movement, political activism in the name of the Church.)

False teachers like to say, "Many denominations preach the Gospel and therefore move people to faith in Christ. Therefore, all confessions are equally good." False teachers fail to distinguish between what is good in the Gospel proclamation and what is bad. For instance, the impact of the Word is more powerful when it is pure. Every denomination has sincere believers, false teachers, and hypocrites who have no faith but pretend to worship. (Two worship professors at Notre Dame were atheists.) The less we toy with the Word and adulterate it with our own opinions, the more God's Word is allowed to run unfettered, to convert and strengthen hearts.

In contrast, when something begins to invade a denomination, the false teaching quickly takes over with a vengeance. Time after time the same pattern is repeated. For example, Creation is taught for a long time. Then some object and want to evolution a place. Soon evolution is the only doctrine allowed.

One reader sent me an article by someone from the Church of Sweden . The state imposed women's ordination on the Church of Sweden some years ago. The bishops objected and were replaced. Then some bishops remained and supported those who objected to women's ordination. The newly ordained who were a little more conservative were tolerated and protected. But no longer. If a candidate in the Church of Sweden objects to women's ordination, he will not become a pastor.

That is just one issue, but it reveals how human reason takes over a church body. In time only human reason is taught and God's Word is never proclaimed. In fact, the most basic doctrines are openly scorned. One LCMS pastor wrote about religion class at his ALC college. The professor denounced all the doctrines of the Bible and said, "There. Lightning didn't strike me." Earlier in time the professor would have been hounded out of the denomination just for admitting lack of faith. But the weeds took over.

The Lutheran-Reformed union denominations are a good example of how God's Word works and yet becomes smothered. The more these groups relied on Luther's doctrine, the longer they remained Christian. Yet in each case they slowly reverted to pure rationalism, Universalism, and Unitarianism. Unitarianism denies the divinity of Christ and most Unitarian ministers are atheists. The conservatives who wanted to teach the existence of God lost out in the 1920s or so. Universalism teaches that everyone is already saved.

Noteworthy in this lesson is that the corrupt tree is cut down. The false teacher will receive more pay and more glory in this life than all the faithful ministers put together. But he will be cut down in time. He will die eternally and be gathered into the place prepared for him – an eternity of Hell where his body and soul will suffer the torments of living according to man's plan instead of God's.

In a few verses Jesus also observes that Judgment Day will have many people saying, "Lord Lord, did we not teach in Your Name and cast out devils, and do many signs and wonders IN YOUR NAME?" Jesus' response is "Get out of here. I never knew you, you workers of iniquity."

The Jehovah's Witnesses told me angrily that they were teaching the Gospel all over the community and what was I doing? I said, "We teach all over the world." That only made them angrier.

Fuller Seminary had a class called Signs and Wonders, as if they wanted to remind Jesus of what He warned us about so many years ago. And the School of Missions also taught that faith in Christ was not necessary or even good. I wonder if they put that statement in the fund-raising literature?

We can say the words and go through the motions all we want, but God alone can judge our hearts. If we fool all of mankind, we still do not have the wisdom to fool God. He is not mocked. Whatever a man sows, he will reap in abundance.

Although this lesson gives us a perfect picture of the difference between sound and false doctrine, we also need to pay attention to the confidence taught in sound doctrine. Every denomination would agree about false teachers (however they define them). But what about the good tree? Do they trust the good tree completely? They do not understand at all that the Word alone will bring about all that God wills. Sadly, many or most Lutherans do not believe this today.

In gardening, 99% of the work consists of this – getting the right seed, the right stock, the right bulbs. I can buy a squishy, half rotted, small daffodil bulb for a certain amount of money. I have done it. And then I look with astonishment at the pathetic daffodil that emerges from the ground, looking carsick. Or I can buy a daffodil so fat and healthy that three plants are joined together. Ten bulbs are really 30 flowers. They are so packed with nutrition that they beg to be planted in the ground.

So is the pure Word of God. It is so powerful that as soon as it appears, the devils of this world quake and rage. They only have to glimpse it and their lupine fangs come out. But at the same time, this Word of God powerfully comforts the weak and contrite sinner. Experience shows that most believers are the nothings of this world, scorned, disabled in many cases, lacking in political and economic power. Satan would like these weak people to tumble over and fall for his word, but he rages that they cling to the truth.

Even the weak and frail produce amazing miracles through the Word of God and this spectacle further enrages the demons, "who believe but their hide bristles." But we should not look for the fruit of the Gospel and the power of the Word in bricks and endowments. The Holy Spirit is powerful in working without the trappings of earthly power and uniquely through the Means of Grace.

A man can open a frail old hymnal (The Lutheran Hymnal) or an ancient KJV and find more wisdom from God than everything taught in the seminaries today.

One of my greatest pleasures is having someone phone and start talking about the great wisdom and comfort found in the Book of Concord, itself a miracle of unity and expression. Some will say, "Did you know this?" And read a favorite passage. The Book of Concord is the fruit of the faith of the Confessors. We can see that the six men who gave us the Book of Concord were concerned about the truth of the Gospel and not their own comfort. They all suffered great privation at different times. Not one of them could say, "Hey, do you know who I used to be?"

As we read the Book of Concord we can judge the tree by the fruit we see. And we can say, "These were not wolves in sheep's clothing, but men who confessed the truth at a difficult time. May we be as faithful as they were. Amen."

Martin Luther's Gospel Admonition

"Now, the Lord in this passage speaks, in particular, of preachers or prophets, whose real and proper fruit is nothing else than this, that they diligently proclaim this will of God to the people and teach them that God is gracious and merciful and has no pleasure in the death of a sinner, but wants him to live, moreover, that God has manifested His mercy by having His only-begotten Son become man. Whoever, now, receives Him and believes in Him, that is, whoever takes comfort in the fact that for the sake of His Son, God will be merciful to him, will forgive his sins, and grant him eternal salvation, etc., — *whoever is engaged in this preaching of the pure Gospel and thus directs men to Christ, the only Mediator between God and men, he, as a preacher, is doing the will of God*. That is the genuine fruit by which no one is deceived or duped. For if it were possible that the devil were to preach this truth, the preaching would not be false or made up of lies and a person believing it would have what it promises.— *After* this fruit, which is the *principal and most reliable one* and cannot deceive, there follow in the course of time other fruits, namely, a life in beautiful harmony with this doctrine and in no way contrary to it. But these fruits are *to be regarded as genuine fruits only where the first fruit*, namely, *the doctrine of Christ*, already exists." (Walther, *The Proper Distinction between Law and Gospel*, p. 413. Matthew 7:21. [emphasis in original]

The Sacraments

God chose to bind His promises to visible signs, sacraments, so that the visual reminders throughout Creation would call man back to the Promises bound with them. The rainbow was the first, when God promised that He would never again destroy the earth with a flood. Every rainbow should refresh that Promise and many other Promises in our minds. The Passover Meal and Exodus are so full of symbols of Christ that a catechism student said, "Every answer is Jesus." Some of them are:

1. The burning bush as the Two Natures of Christ.

2. The cross of blood which made the angel of death pass over the homes suitably prepared with the seal of God's Promise.

3. The serpent raised on wooden stake to heal the people.

4. The bread from heaven.

5. The water from the rock.

6. The Promised Land.

Holy Communion is a combination of Promises from the Old Testament and Jesus' own commands. Each communion service unites us with the work of God from ages ago; so far back we can hardly comprehend that age. And yet, we receive the Living Bread from heaven. The Blood of the innocent Lamb is ours to take away our sin, to give us forgiveness and eternal life.

Although people have complained about the abundance of forgiveness offered in Christian teaching, the over-supply is consistent with Creation.

First of all, God binds His Holy Spirit to His Word so that there is never any doubt about the divine effectiveness of His Word. God either converts or hardens, enlightens or blinds through His Word. The hardening and blinding are the fault of man, who makes himself worse whenever he scoffs at and rejects the Word of God, but they still reveal the power of the Word.

Secondly, God only desires to save, to free man from sin, to provide eternal life, so He provides an abundance of His Word and connects His Word to visible instruments. The Word is the same Word when taught in its purity, whether read, remembered, or spoken. The Gospel Promises create and strengthen faith, whether connected with the spoken Word or the instruments of Holy Baptism and Holy Communion.

God should not be blamed for giving us visible signs of His grace. Most Christians appreciate the meaning of the rainbow, the first connection between a visible sign and God's Promises. Every baptism reminds us of the associations we have with washing, purity, rebirth, and new life. The water of Holy Baptism brings to mind Noah's Ark saving his family from destruction, the life-giving water Moses found for the Israelites, the woman at the well listening to Jesus about, the pool of Siloam giving sight to the blind, and many other Biblical images.

The images of bread and wine are so universal that people around the world connect them to the basics of life. When the manna fell from heaven to feed the Israelites, the nation was being prepared to understand the One who came from above. Nothing is more satisfying to the hungry person than bread, so Jesus gave Himself as the Bread of Life. The Feeding of the Five Thousand is fundamental to our understanding of the divine power of Jesus, but the miracle also illustrates how Jesus could provide His body and blood to believers through Holy Communion across the centuries.

The wine of Holy Communion is associated with the most basic drink of the Bible and the blood of atoning sacrifices. The vineyards and the winepresses worked for centuries prepared people to understand and believe that they would receive the blood of Christ in the sacrament, poured out for the forgiveness of their sins. Animal sacrifice for centuries pointed toward the final and complete sacrifice of the Lamb of God. Blood atonement through animals aided in teaching the Atonement of Christ. Enacting the Last Supper makes each individual a participant in receiving the Visible Word and appreciating its significance.

The Last Supper

The Flood, Our Faith, and Science

Those who enjoy reading about science and ancient mysteries realize that modern man faces a bewildering array of unsolvable mysteries, given our current attitude toward the age and history of the universe. The educational channels solve these problems by proposing that men from Mars created these puzzles. Below are just a few to consider:

Monumental and Technological Marvels of the Past

The Great Pyramid remains one of the tallest structures in the world, at 481 feet, compared to the Gateway Arch in St. Louis, which is 630 feet. The precision of the Great Pyramid's alignment (north-south-east-west) has never been matched. Its construction remains a mystery. Those who propose slave labor carving enormous blocks must explain how men rolled 120 ton stones up ramps. The waste from the carving has not been found. Others argue for casting of the blocks with a concrete mixture. No one really knows the date or origin of the Great Pyramid, which is dated around 2,000 BC. Giant pyramid structures have been found all over the world, and they are often far more massive than the Great Pyramid, which contains 6.5 million tons of material. Some are in China. Others are in Mexico.

In 1911, Yale professor Hiram Bingham found the amazing, forgotten mountain city of Machu Pichu in Peru, a site proving that ancient people built enormous stone structures with incredible precision. The polygonal stone joints will not allow a knife blade to be inserted. How did they construct this city at 8,000 feet with such large stones, without mortar? The website below attributes Machu Pichu to the late Inca period, around 1450 AD.

The Nasca giant animal drawings in Peru went undiscovered until a plane spotted them in the 1920's. No one knows the exact purpose of the 300 drawings spread over 400 square miles of desert, but one thing is clear they can only be viewed from the air. They are dated variously between 200 AD and 1000 AD.

Maps Require Accurate Chronometers

Another enigma is the problem of ancient maps. Ships without accurate charts run aground or get lost and never return. In 1707 Admiral Shovel ran aground with his ships, losing 2,000 men and the admiral himself, a no nonsense officer who hanged the sailor who argued about where they were. Just about the only way to draw a good map is with a precise clock. It is exceedingly difficult to find the longitude without a precise timepiece. This problem became so acute for the British that they offered a reward for the first person to invent a reliable chronometer for ships. The Board of Longitude finally awarded the complete prize to John Harrison in 1773.

Some are saying, "And?" Here is the problem. We have ancient maps drawn with great precision. The most puzzling is an accurate map of the landmass beneath the ice of Antarctica, dated 1532 AD, but based upon earlier maps.

We now have plenty of physical evidence that the Chinese discovered America around 1421 when their fleet of 500 ships circumnavigated the world. Columbus and Magellan both depended upon maps and settled the nerves of their sailors by saying, in effect, "I know where we are. I have maps."

Debunking the Modern Myth

Many of us were trained as if technology came into being with the Industrial Age. We were taught to look down upon the ancients as primitive, illiterate people who knew no creature comforts and had few skills. Whether we visit Sedona or the Grand Canyon, watch Discovery or Animal Planet, stop at a zoo or a natural history museum, we always hear that the universe is billions of years old, that everything has slowly evolved until now. The Genesis Flood is not worth debating because it has been deliberately forgotten, as the Scriptures promised:

For this they willingly are ignorant of, that by the word of God the heavens were of old, and the earth standing out of the water and in the water: 6Whereby the world that then was, being overflowed with water, perished: 7 But the heavens and the earth, which are now, by the same word are kept in store, reserved unto fire against the day of judgment and perdition of ungodly men. 2 Peter 3:5-7

We cannot understand our world or our Christian faith apart from an appreciation of the Flood. Living in this current age without acknowledging the Flood is like going to Niagara and ignoring Niagara Falls. Teaching the Christian faith without the Flood is tantamount to denying the efficacy of the Word.

Alfred Rehwinkel's *The Flood in the Light of the Bible, Geology, and Archaeology* is an essential book for understanding the Genesis Flood..

We have no reason to use science to prove that the Bible is actually correct. Instead we can use the most common observations of science and history to shed light on the miraculous depth of God's Word. Luther compared study of the Bible to a gold mine where the veins run in all directions. The more gold we take from the Bible, the more we realize how much remains.

The earth is young and recorded history is fairly recent. Why is it that everything in history is vague before 2,000 BC? The Great Pyramid is dated as existing in 2,000 BC, but no one is sure. In fact, no one knows the purpose of the Great Pyramid. If it is the mausoleum of a great king, then they forgot to put the body inside when they sealed it up.

God created Adam and Eve in 4004 BC, as calculated from the chronologies in the Bible. They sinned and were driven out of Paradise (Iraq). In our minds the Flood came next, but an entire world civilization grew across the globe, supported by the luxuriant growth of vegetation, an abundant supply of animals and minerals.

The Flood is commonly dated around 2300-2500 BC. That means mankind had 15 centuries to be fruitful and fill the earth. That time period was more than enough to fill the earth with billions of people. Several factors would have helped:

1. The climate was ideal, without seasons.
2. Men lived as long as 1000 years (Methuselah).
3. Living conditions would have promoted large families and decreased death due to famine and plague.

All civilizations have stories of a golden age followed by a global flood where one family was spared and subsequently replenished the earth. Liberals view this fact as proving that the Bible borrowed the stories and invented Noah and the ark, failing to see how pagans remembered the truth and retold the story in their own way, a bit distorted but remarkably close to the Genesis account.

The Pre-Flood World Mineral Abundance

We can make several assumptions about the pre-Flood world. We know that minerals were simply lying on top of the earth to be picked up and used. There are modern examples of such abundance. The mining town of Jerome, Arizona was developed because American Indians knew they could pick up raw copper on Mt. Mingus. The simple mining methods of the 19 th century dug billions of dollars of copper, silver, and gold from that mountain. However, the Indians got what they needed from the surface. The California gold rush began when gold was found at Sutter's Mill. Early gold-miners simply panned the stream for flecks of gold.

Balmy Climate

Seasons did not develop until after the Flood, so the pre-Flood world was uniformly watered by a mist. The climate was warm and balmy; people were spared our violent weather caused by distribution of heat (hurricanes) and clashes of cold fronts with hot, humid weather (tornados). We know that plant and animal life was super-abundant because the fossil record preserved by the Flood shows tropical plants and animals evenly distributed across the globe, including such harsh places as Siberia . The combination of warm weather and abundant moisture meant that crops grew easily, that men did not wear themselves out through labor, that people obtained plenty of nutrition from their food. After the Flood, the only places supporting a large population were those areas where food production was remarkably efficient. Before the Flood, this was true throughout the planet.

Technology

Most importantly, man developed remarkable technology before the Flood because of his longevity, his relative ease in producing food, and the mineral resources available. The effect of a longer life has already been seen in this last century. Social Security was established with the assumption of retired people living one year past their entitlement age of 65. Now those who reach 65 can expect to live to the age of 85 and be active most of those years. My sainted mother traveled all over the world (including Machu Pichu) after retirement, living in Davenport, St. Louis, New Ulm, and Glendale. Before the Flood, when men lived to be almost 1,000 years old, they had time to accumulate astonishing skills and train others for many generations. When the World Trade Center collapsed on the heroic firemen of New York City, it was said in the press that these highly trained men were simply irreplaceable because of their decades of experience with specialized equipment and unique situations.

One Modern Man

A few people realize the impact of one brilliant man pursuing his ideas in technology. The world advanced very little in technology between the time of the Roman Empire and the 1856 birth of Nicola Tesla, the son of a Serbian orthodox priest. Scientists knew about electricity, but Tesla invented the alternating current generator and trounced the DC generating schemes of his former employer, the great inventor Thomas

Edison. Tesla wired the Chicago Exposition, built the generators for Niagara Falls, and invented radio, only to see the Nobel Prize go to Marconi, who used 14 Tesla patents to make his radio work. Tesla was constantly hampered by lab fires, financial troubles, and opposition to his genius, but he won 700 patents for his technological genius. Tesla laid the foundation for television, laser weapons, and remotely guided weapons.

If we look at the technological progress of the last 90 years, we can easily talk to people who remember having their farms wired for electricity, who recall seeing their first horseless carriage, who flew to Europe on a jet and used a computer to send email to friends. Germany still relied on horses at the end of WWII, even though they were competing with America to build a nuclear bomb and the first military jets. Therefore, it is not unlikely that the pre-Flood world enjoyed the same burst of technological progress. Much of this knowledge could have accompanied Noah on the ark. Nostalgia about the Golden Age before the Flood is recorded in this brief and often misunderstood account.

Hints of the Pre-Flood Glory

And the whole earth was of one language, and of one speech. 2 And it came to pass, as they journeyed from the east, that they found a plain in the land of Shinar; and they dwelt there. 3 And they said one to another, Go to, let us make brick, and burn them throughly. And they had brick for stone, and slime had they for morter. 4 And they said, Go to, let us build us a city and a tower, whose top may reach unto heaven; and let us make us a name, lest we be scattered abroad upon the face of the whole earth. 5 And the LORD came down to see the city and the tower, which the children of men builded. 6 And the LORD said, Behold, the people is one, and they have all one language; and this they begin to do: and now nothing will be restrained from them, which they have imagined to do. 7 Go to, let us go down, and there confound their language, that they may not understand one another's speech. 8 So the LORD scattered them abroad from thence upon the face of all the earth: and they left off to build the city. 9 Therefore is the name of it called Babel; because the LORD did there confound the language of all the earth: and from thence did the LORD scatter them abroad upon the face of all the earth. Genesis 11:1-9

The Tower of Babel follows the death Noah (at the age of 950) and the genealogies of Genesis 10. Why did they want to reach into heaven? Had men been there before? We should not rule out any capacity of man before the Flood, given our own progress in the last 50 years. All theories about men from Mars can just as easily be turned into ones about earthmen on Mars. Nevertheless, God has good reasons to limit our knowledge of the pre-Flood world. We should remember instead that the Flood is a constant reminder of what went wrong in that era.

Modern Parallels

And it came to pass, when men began to multiply on the face of the earth, and daughters were born unto them, 2 That the sons of God saw the daughters of men that they were fair; and they took them wives of all which they chose. 3 And the LORD said, My spirit shall not always strive with man, for that he also is flesh: yet his days shall be an hundred and twenty years. 4 There were giants in the earth in those days; and also after that, when the sons of God came in unto the daughters of men, and they bare children to them, the same became mighty men which were of old, men of renown. 5 And GOD saw that the wickedness of man was great in the earth, and that every imagination of the thoughts of his heart was only evil continually. Genesis 6:1-5

If we understand "sons of God" to be the believers who were trained to be faithful to the Word, then this passage loses its mystery. Instead of marrying believers, the prosperous men in the pre-Flood era considered physical beauty more important than faith in God, so they increased the numbers of pagans as their religious indifference grew. God said He would not always strive against man to keep him on the straight and narrow. The giants in the earth were the ferocious tyrants of the ancient era. The marriage of believers (sons of God) to unbelievers (daughters of men) led to the birth of godless, powerful men. Mankind degenerated so much that every thought was wicked.

And it repented the LORD that he had made man on the earth, and it grieved him at his heart. 7 And the LORD said, I will destroy man whom I have created from the face of the earth; both man, and beast, and the creeping thing, and the fowls of the air; for it repenteth me that I have made them. 8 But Noah found grace in the eyes of the LORD. 9 These are the generations of Noah: Noah was a just man and perfect in his generations, and Noah walked with God. Genesis 6:6-9

Our country – our whole world – seems to be eagerly following the pattern of the pre-Flood era.
• Christian leaders and laity are zealous in expressing their approval of pagan religions.

- As one commentator noted recently, the cathedrals of France are empty, except for tourists, while 5 million Muslim adherents in France worship fervently and fruitfully multiply. The dominant social factor in all of Europe is the fast-growing group of Muslim teen-agers.
- Conservative Lutherans in America, once a respected religious force, are so weak today that they could not knock the skin off a pudding.
- Phoenix reached a new low in having a Catholic diocese so lax that Boston's Cardinal Law sent some of his worst pedophile priests here. Phoenix Bishop O'Brien welcomed them and obstructed justice – a felony – when the priests got caught. Bishop O'Brien is now famous for signing a confession of sorts, fighting against it in public, and then running from a car accident in which he ran down and killed a carpenter.

People are tired of hearing warnings, but this one should be heeded:

But as the days of Noe were, so shall also the coming of the Son of man be. 38 For as in the days that were before the flood they were eating and drinking, marrying and giving in marriage, until the day that Noe entered into the ark, 39 And knew not until the flood came, and took them all away; so shall also the coming of the Son of man be. Matthew 24:37-39

Ecclesiastical leaders should be especially mindful of this admonition:

For the time is come that judgment must begin at the house of God: and if it first begin at us, what shall the end be of them that obey not the gospel of God? 1 Peter 4:1

The Genesis Flood

Noah was once called the least successful preacher of righteousness in the history of the world. However, his denomination did not shrink under his leadership, in marked contrast to the Church Growth leaders of the LCMS and WELS. I would like to think that Noah borrowed heavily to build the ark, only to see his loans, notes, and debentures liquidated, but we have no record of Noah's debts.

And Noah begat three sons, Shem, Ham, and Japheth. 11 The earth also was corrupt before God, and the earth was filled with violence. 12 And God looked upon the earth, and, behold, it was corrupt; for all flesh had corrupted his way upon the earth. 13 And God said unto Noah, The end of all flesh is come before me; for the earth is filled with violence through them; and, behold, I will destroy them with the earth. 14 Make thee an ark of gopher wood; rooms shalt thou make in the ark, and shalt pitch it within and without with pitch. Genesis 6:10-14

Noah built the ark, which was the largest ship created until modern times. It was not a cute little tug with giraffe and sheep smiling out the windows, but a small, squat battleship-sized vessel. The size depends on the length of the Biblical cubit. The ark was between 450 and 600 feet long. Few people realize how much volume a ship of that size can carry. Nevertheless, problems remain for the rationalist. Children wonder about feeding and mucking that many animals. How could a family of eight keep up? Just as God commanded the Flood through His efficacious Word, He also gathered the animals for the ark through His Word. Whatever needs the animals had could have been provided through His Word as well. Some propose that the animals spent their time in a state of hibernation. We should emphasize that God provided for them, even as He does now. If someone spends just a little time with God's Creation, the wonders seen on a daily basis will quench any need for rationalistic answers. How can an ugly monarch caterpillar feed on dreadful milkweed leaves, fatten up, and sudden create a "jade coffin with golden nails"? When we lived in New Ulm, we adopted two monarch caterpillars we named Koenig and Tiefel. Suddenly one night each bloated caterpillar turned into a beautiful chrysalis. The "golden nails" looked like real gold. Later the shape and color of the monarch wings could be seen through the delicate green wall of the chrysalis. Soon a monarch emerged, dried off, and took flight. In Phoenix we have viceroys instead of monarchs. Predators see the monarch coloration of the viceroy and avoid it, since milkweed-fed monarchs taste awful to birds. No one can explain how the caterpillar turns into its own transformation machine and then into a butterfly, nor can anyone figure out how or why the viceroy decided to mock the monarch.

The Flood was not a local disaster, as the apostates still insist today, but a vast global catastrophe. We have all seen what a shift in the weather can do with the El Nino and El Nina effects. Picture this probable scenario on a global scale, all accomplished through God's will and command, His efficacious Word:

- The mantle of moisture watering the earth lost its equilibrium and turned into rain - "and the windows of heaven were opened." Genesis 7:11
- Volcanoes burst through the earth, producing an enormous volume of steam, as they still do today.
- Earthquakes pushed up the ocean floor and send tsunamis across the land. In the six hundredth year of Noah's life, in the second month, the seventeenth day of the month, the same day were all the fountains of the great deep broken up.... Genesis 7:11

God caused the rain to fall 40 days and nights. The water rose up for 150 days. Those of us who went through the great flood of 1993 remember 60 days of rain and the rising of the Mississippi. Bridges closed. Streets were under water. Dikes were destroyed to flood thousands of acres of farmland, to spare the cities and especially St. Louis. For a long time it seemed as if the flood would never end. The reek of the flood lasted a long time afterwards, with bloated farm animals floating like enormous balloons on the filthy water.

The Genesis flood covered all the land masses, even the mountain tops by 15 cubits.

Fifteen cubits upward did the waters prevail; and the mountains were covered. Genesis 7:20

One can well imagine the effect of the rising waters. Every living thing headed for higher ground. This gathering forced predators from a wide area together with their prey. The common fear felt by the smaller animals toward the predators was overwhelmed by the panic caused by the rising waters. The result should have been high ground where thousands of animals died together with an unusually high percentage of predators. As Rehwinkel shows, there are many elevated locations where fissures are filled to a depth of 300 feet with shattered bones of animals. An island near Corfu is called the mountain of bones because of the bones from its base to its peak. (Rehwinkel, p. 180)

Fossil Fuels

Our discussions about energy betray one of the most important effects of the Flood. Everyday the environmentalists worry about the depletion of fossil fuels: coal, oil, and natural gas. As I learned in grammar school, coal is formed from vast amounts of pressure and heat upon plant material. Leaf-prints are often found embedded in lumps of coal. Oil in Michigan is associated with brine, the residue of a vast sea that once covered the area. Brine encouraged Dow to move to Midland, Michigan, to make chemicals. Brine-wells still dot the area. Oil from Michigan is high in salt and corrodes pipes quickly. Oil deposits are also associated with vast shoals of suddenly killed fish.

The fossils found in rocks are additional footprints of the Flood. Science teachers seldom tell us that animals and plants do not turn into stone when they die. They rot while being eaten by the creatures appointed by God to recycle the elements: molds, bacteria, springtails, sowbugs, pillbugs, maggots, centipedes, millipedes, and earthworms. Fossils can only be formed under special circumstances: heat, pressure, and an abundance of minerals. The global distribution of fossils is another reminder of the global catastrophe.

Dinosaurs

Dinosaurs are supposed to be the poster boys of evolution. According to old earth advocates, dinosaurs evolved until they suddenly died off in a great cataclysm. A comet or meteorite strike is currently popular as the bell-ringer for all dinosaurs. Let us pause to enjoy the picture – once offered – of newly evolved rodents eating all the dinosaur eggs. We realize now that the rodents would have died of high cholesterol from such a rich diet.

The Flood killed all the dinosaurs, except those on Noah's ark and those in the oceans. Dinosaurs have been caught in the ocean recently, so they are not extinct. The land dinosaurs gradually lost ground to the growth of human civilization, leaving behind stories of flying dragons. Marco Polo saw dinosaurs in China . Also, the post-Flood shift in weather did not allow for the luxuriant growth that once fed the dinosaurs. Doubtless the cold weather also made it difficult for the large dinosaurs to adjust.

Dinosaur bones are often found in vast amounts together, washed together in a jumble. For the bones to turn into stone and be jumbled together, all the actions of the Flood are required.

Geography

The geography of our planet betrays the muddy footprints of the Flood. Vast deposits of clay can only be explained as the result of inundation. The red rock formations of Sedona are crowned with ocean fossils at the highest level. The Great Lakes draining into the Gulf of Mexico through the Mississippi River are so exquisitely poised that slightly different circumstances would have emptied them instead of giving us a vast source of fresh water, fish, and navigation.

Science teachers patiently explained to me and others that the Colorado River spent millions of years creating the Grand Canyon. The features of the canyon match the results of a rapid scouring by a vast flood pouring through the area. Flood waters pick up rocks and debris, turning the stream of water into an irresistible force. Our pool pump picks up gravel and moves it around like popcorn. A flood does the same for boulders, rocks, and sand.

Scientists today remain puzzled by many features of our planet. Charles Darwin saw many signs of a battered and bruised earth on his lengthy voyage, even while developing his version of evolution. Many modern explanations strike me more as deus ex machina than the Biblical version, which is commonly mocked. The glaciers are the secular substitutes for the Flood. The anonymous comet is another cause, when Martians do not fit the scenario. Immanuel Velikovsy had some strange ideas, but he was instrumental in getting people to realize that the ancient stories of global catastrophes were rooted in fact.

Collapse of Technologies in the Past

Noah and his sons lived out the enormous life-spans granted before the Flood. Now people laugh at Methuselah living to be 969 years, Noah having children at the age of 500. People seldom think about Noah and his sons living into the modern age, bringing pre-Flood technology with them, and that technology collapsing after the men of the Golden Age were gone. Many assume that man gets more skilled as the years go by. The history we know tells me that civilizations are more likely to collapse, only to have primitives wandering around the glorious but misunderstood monuments of a previous age. Arizona once supported a large Indian nation that used irrigation canals, that had many skills and crafts. Did the Hohokam move away or did an extensive drought destroy the cohesiveness and drive of the nation?

Implications for Today

God gave the rainbow as the visible sign of His promise never to flood the earth again. Therefore, many view the rainbow as the first sacrament.

I do set my bow in the cloud, and it shall be for a token of a covenant between me and the earth. 14 And it shall come to pass, when I bring a cloud over the earth, that the bow shall be seen in the cloud: 15 And I will remember my covenant, which is between me and you and every living creature of all flesh; and the waters shall no more become a flood to destroy all flesh. 16 And the bow shall be in the cloud; and I will look upon it, that I may remember the everlasting covenant between God and every living creature of all flesh that is upon the earth. Genesis 9:13-16

For this is as the waters of Noah unto me: for as I have sworn that the waters of Noah should no more go over the earth; so have I sworn that I would not be wroth with thee, nor rebuke thee. Isaiah 54:9

Now the rainbow is favored as the symbol of the occult, often found on cars with unicorn stickers, and as the logo of multi-centralism.
The seasons were established:
While the earth remaineth, seedtime and harvest, and cold and heat, and summer and winter, and day and night shall not cease. Genesis 8:22
Just as nitrogen replaces oxygen in a chemical plant, preventing fire and explosions, so the environmental movement has replaced and supplanted God's Creation as motivation for our care of the earth.
Who changed the truth of God into a lie, and worshipped and served the creature more than the Creator, who is blessed forever. Amen. Romans 1:25
The countries where Marxism flourished have destroyed vast areas of the countryside with their nuclear waste and accidents (Russia), their misuse and manipulation of the land (Aral Sea, Russia), and their self-important projects (Three Gorges Dam, China). Enormous areas of China and Africa are evolving into desert. Perhaps man should use some introspection when blaming God for so much harm in this world.

rain

Holy Baptism

Jesus mentioned Noah in His warnings about the Judgment, but we should also remember Noah's ark being the symbol of Holy Baptism in 1 Peter. This particular passage is so clear about the efficacy of baptism that most of the revisions of the King James Version, while stating their desire to remain true to the original, consciously avoid the plain meaning of the passage. As Martin Jackson said about the Baptist editors of the modern KJV Bibles, "They know their customers." What is this offending passage, that must be modified, bent, and twisted in all the modern versions?

Which sometime were disobedient, when once the longsuffering of God waited in the days of Noah, while the ark was a preparing, wherein few, that is, eight souls were saved by water. 21 The like figure whereunto even baptism doth also now save us (not the putting away of the filth of the flesh, but the answer of a good conscience toward God,) by the resurrection of Jesus Christ: 22 Who is gone into heaven, and is on the right hand of God; angels and authorities and powers being made subject unto him. 1 Peter 3:20-22

Holy Baptism is like Noah's ark, saving us when the world is threatened by a vast, destructive flood of political and religious propaganda. Rehwinkel theorizes that the shape of Noah's ark was squat and rounded, like the *kuffa* still being used today by primitive tribes, a ship useless for speed but almost impossible to capsize. Holy Baptism is not glamorous and exciting – we never see one on religious TV – but God's promise remains with the water and the Word.

The Flood should remind us always about the power of God's Word to destroy what is evil and the efficacy of God's Word in saving us through the merits of Jesus Christ.

The Genesis Flood and Creation

When we look at the world around us, we are really looking at two manifestations of His power in the Creating Word: Creation itself and the world shaped by the Genesis Flood. Although the wise men of the age willingly overlook the obvious, scraps of history confirm what the Bible reveals.

Enormous precious gems gathered by hand seem to be the ingredients of a magical story, yet the Robin Fox biography of Alexander the Great records that the Greek soldiers came across an area near India where no one was aware of the value of gems. They found them in great abundance and gathered up the treasure. Likewise, people in the past have found large gold nuggets, deposits of silver slabs, and enormous diamonds within easy reach.

Coal was discovered in America when a man built a fire under a cliff and set the hill on fire. He was not aware that his cliff was solid anthracite, the hardest and best type of coal. The coal, oil, and natural gas companies should really be called Genesis Flood Deposits, since their fossil fuels continue to give energy to the entire world. How novel it would be if the geologists of the world said, "When God renewed the world with the global Flood, He also provided for its future needs with gigantic supplies of carbon-based fuel."

"And this our life, exempt from public haunts, finds tongues in trees, books in running brooks, sermons in stones and good in everything." (Shakespeare, As You Like it)

Everything we love and value in this world is designed and fashioned by God, through Jesus, the creating Word. The teaching of Jesus is so filled with images from His Creation that all the plants and animals continue this teaching, reminding us of the wisdom of God.

The love which we value is first of all God's love, exemplified in the giving of His beloved Son to die for our sins and rise to eternal life. The life God gives us is just a foretaste of the eternal life won for us in the death and resurrection of our Savior. All the sins of mankind were paid by

Him on the cross, just as all the promises of the Old Testament were fulfilled in Him.

To gather His Creation into the Kingdom, God gave us the revelation of His will in the Scriptures, and united His Holy Spirit with the Word so that we will never doubt its efficacy. He also united His Gospel promises with the most basic elements of nature to give us concrete examples of cleansing and forgiveness.

> Hast thou not known? hast thou not heard,
> *that* the everlasting God, the LORD, the Creator of the ends of the earth,
> fainteth not, neither is weary?
> *there is* no searching of his understanding.
> 29 He giveth power to the faint;
> and to *them that have* no might
> he increaseth strength.
> 30 Even the youths shall faint and be weary,
> and the young men shall utterly fall:
> 31 But they that wait upon the LORD
> shall renew *their* strength;
> they shall mount up with wings as eagles;
> they shall run, and not be weary;
> *and* they shall walk, and not faint.
> Isaiah 40:28-31

Divine Plan

When God gave life to Adam and Eve, He placed them in an earthly paradise, which foreshadowed that eternal life which was freely offered in the Gospel Promises of a Savior, even after our First Parents sinned and lost the Garden of Eden. The proclamation of this Good News, which began with Genesis 3:15, continued throughout the Old Testament. As many as believed in Him were counted as sons of God and given eternal life.

Noah preached this righteousness through faith.

And spared not the old world, but saved Noah the eighth *person*, a preacher of righteousness, bringing in the flood upon the world of the ungodly; 2 Peter 2:5

Abraham was justified by faith and became the example for all those who would be justified by faith.

And he brought him forth abroad, and said, Look now toward heaven, and tell the stars, if thou be able to number them: and he said unto him, So shall thy seed be. 6 And he believed in the LORD; and he counted it to him for righteousness. Genesis 15:5

And the father of circumcision to them who are not of the circumcision only, but who also walk in the steps of that faith of our father Abraham, which *he had* being *yet* uncircumcised. 13 For the promise, that he should be the heir of the world, *was* not to Abraham, or to his seed, through the law, but through the righteousness of faith. Romans 4:12-13

Moses has been identified exclusively with the Law, but this hero of religion should been seen as a man of faith, a believer in the coming Messiah.

By faith Moses, when he was born, was hid three months of his parents, because they saw *he was* a proper child; and they were not afraid of the king's commandment. 24 By faith Moses, when he was come to years, refused to be called the son of Pharaoh's daughter; 25 Choosing rather to suffer affliction with the people of God, than to enjoy the pleasures of sin for a season; 26 Esteeming the reproach of Christ greater riches than the treasures in Egypt: for he had respect unto the recompense of the reward. 27 By faith he forsook Egypt, not fearing the wrath of the king: for he endured, as seeing him who is invisible. 28 Through faith he kept the passover, and the sprinkling of blood, lest he that destroyed the firstborn should touch them. 29 By faith they passed through the Red sea as by dry *land* : which the Egyptians assaying to do were drowned. Hebrews 11:23-29

And were all baptized unto Moses in the cloud and in the sea; 3 And did all eat the same spiritual meat; 4 And did all drink the same spiritual drink: for they drank of that spiritual Rock that followed them: and that Rock was Christ. 1 Corinthians 10:2-4

Job lost his children, his property, and his health, scraping his sores while his comforters besieged him with accusations and his wife shouted, "Curse God and die." Nevertheless, Job believed in Christ:

For I know *that* my redeemer liveth, and *that* he shall stand at the latter *day* upon the earth: 26 And *though* after my skin *worms* destroy this *body* , yet in my flesh shall I see God: 27 Whom I shall see for myself, and mine eyes shall behold, and not another; *though* my reins be consumed within me. Job 19:25-27

From the beginning of time, the Lord of Creation has gathered His elect into the Kingdom of God, and bestowed the fruit of the Christian faith upon them. When time comes to an end on the Day of Judgment, there will be a new heaven and a new earth, with the heavenly Jerusalem descending in glory.

And he carried me away in the spirit to a great and high mountain, and shewed me that great city, the holy Jerusalem, descending out of heaven from God, 11 Having the glory of God: and her light *was* like unto a stone most precious, even like a jasper stone, clear as crystal; 12 And had a wall great and high, *and* had twelve gates, and at the gates twelve angels, and names written thereon, which are *the names* of the twelve tribes of the children of Israel: 13 On the east three gates; on the north three gates; on the south three gates; and on the west three gates. 14 And the wall of the city had twelve foundations, and in them the names of the twelve apostles of the Lamb. Revelation 21:1-14

Jerusalem the Golden

Jerusalem the golden,
With milk and honey blest,
Beneath thy contemplation
Sink heart and voice opprest.
I know not, oh, I know not,
What joys await us there,
What radiancy of glory,
What bliss beyond compare.

They stand, those halls of Zion ,
All jubilant with song
And bright with many an angel
And all the martyr throng.
The Prince is ever in them;
The daylight is serene;
The pastures of the blessed

Are decked in glorious sheen.

There is the throne of David;
And there, from care released,
The shout of them that triumph,
The song of them that feast;
And they who with their Leader
Have conquered in the fight
Forever and forever
Are clad in robes of white.

O sweet and blessed country,
The home of God's elect!
O sweet and blessed country
That eager hearts expect!
Jesus, in mercy bring us
To that dear land of rest,
Who art, with God the Father
And Spirit, ever blest.

(Hymn #613, *The Lutheran Hymnal*)

The Eagle